Introducing the Uncommon Lectionary

Opening the
Bible to
Seekers
and
Disciples

Thomas G. Bandy

ABINGDON PRESS
NASHVILLE

INTRODUCING THE UNCOMMON LECTIONARY
OPENING THE BIBLE TO SEEKERS AND DISCIPLES

This book is printed on acid-free paper.

Library of Congress Cataloging-in-Publication Data

Bandy, Thomas G., 1950-
    Introducing the uncommon lectionary : opening the Bible to seekers and disciples / Thomas G. Bandy.
        p. cm.
    ISBN 0-687-49627-6 (binding: adhesive, pbk. : alk. paper)
    1. Public worship. 2. Common lectionary (1992) 3. Bible—Liturgical lessons, English. I. Title.
    BV15.B36 2006
    264'.34—dc22

                                                                        2005030967

06 07 08 09 10 11 12 13 14 15—10 9 8 7 6 5 4 3 2 1

MANUFACTURED IN THE UNITED STATES OF AMERICA

To my two grandfathers:

To Kenneth Carpenter,

pioneer in teaching English as a
second language; radio and
television entrepreneur, and
founder of WHK in Cleveland,
Ohio; lay leader and spiritual guide
for adult Christian education for
Church of the Savior

To George Bandy,

Hungarian immigrant and crane
operator; Christian model and
mentor to his family and friends; a
witness to the power of endurance
in the face of bigotry and hope in
Jesus Christ

CONTENTS

INTRODUCTION

A New Perspective

Looking Through a Biblical Window
into Contemporary Experience

The story of Jesus' conversation with the woman at the well establishes the context of worship in the contemporary world as no other biblical story can. The basic story is this: Jesus and the disciples are on their way from here to there, and stop briefly at a historic place of spirituality that is now, frankly, going to seed. While the disciples go to the nearby minimart for groceries, Jesus waits beside the well lacking the means to get a drink of water. An ethnic woman (that is, a woman perceived by a dominant culture to be different) comes to the well to draw water. Whenever haves and have-nots meet, there is almost always a conversation, and this is the case here.

Jesus asks for a drink. The woman takes no offense, but expresses surprise. Increasing cultural diversity has escalated bigotry and barriers. "If you knew who I was," Jesus says, "you would ask me for living water, a veritable spring welling up to eternal life." In the bubbling cauldron of spirituality that defines her world, the woman is not particularly amazed at this bizarre language. She takes it in stride and pragmatically speculates how she is to get this living water.

One can imagine a moment of silence. It appears that Jesus and the woman are talking past each other—same terminology, but different meanings. Perhaps a third party will mediate communication. Jesus asks for her husband, knowing full well that in contemporary society over half the people are separated or divorced and living with somebody different and raising somebody else's kids, every few years. The lack of judgment, however, and clear interest in right relationships, lead the woman to ask the question closest to her heart. "You are a prophet!" she exclaims.

Now one might speculate about this. If you thought you had met an authentic prophet, and you had an opportunity to ask just one question, what question would you ask? What is the winning number of the lottery? What will the blood test reveal? Will my children have a good life? Will I find true love? Who will win the war? But the woman goes deeper than all of this. She asks where she should go to meet God. She asks about worship. Where should we worship? Will I find God on the mountain? Will I find God in the temple? Where will I find God—because I desperately, urgently need to be in contact with divinity? That is the deepest, most far-reaching and fundamental question of the seeker society in which we live.

So Jesus tells her. "Woman, believe me, the hour is coming when neither on this mountain nor in Jerusalem will you worship the Father.... The hour is coming, and now is, when the true worshipers will worship the Father in spirit and truth, for such the Father seeks to worship him. God is spirit, and those who worship him must worship in spirit and truth" (John 4:21-24 RSV). Meeting God is not a tactical issue, Jesus says. It is an authenticity issue. It is a matter of absolute sincerity, deep conviction, and surrender of self. That being the case, any tactic will do.

The woman has a follow-up question. Contemporary people *always* have a follow-up question. And Jesus is prepared with a zinger of a comeback. "Who is going to show me what spirit and truth look like?" the woman asks. "Is the Messiah coming?" Jesus takes her breath away by smiling deprecatingly and saying, "Ah, well, that would be me."

The story goes that the woman finds her friends, they all meet Jesus, and many are saved. They've figured out where and how to worship. But the real point of the story is not the reaction of the Samaritans, but the reaction of the disciples—those solid, veteran, dutiful, restless churchmen who were out buying groceries for the journey. They were shocked. Maybe they didn't speak their indignation, but Jesus knew it anyway. "Look, guys," Jesus says. "The harvest is ripe. The seekers are everywhere. Now isn't the time to bring the people to God in worship; now is the time to bring God to the people in worship."

Today this same story is being repeated all around the world, and certainly in North America. The great debate about worship is just as divided about tactics, and just as urgent for seekers, as in ancient times. All the key elements are there:

1. *It's common conversation.* People are talking about God, and how to meet God, in food courts, sports arenas, television talk shows, and pubs. Although the conversation is fragmenting exponentially in all directions, the one emerging consensus is that the one place people are *least* likely to meet God is in an established church.

2. *It's conversation among self-declared outcasts.* There are no ethnic groups today. Everybody is ethnic. There is no normative culture today. Everybody is an outcast. Alienation is rampant, and people quest for quality relationships as Arthur searched for the Holy Grail. Even established church people don't feel "established" anymore, and sense they are outcasts in the world at large and mavericks in their own denominations.

3. *It's about worship.* Behind all the debate, skepticism, posturing indifference, and passionate strategic planning is a vast urgency to meet God. People want to connect with God, sit at the feet of God, learn from God, grow in God, and merge with God. They want God. Whether it is for healing, coaching, celebrating, thanking, vindicating, or just hanging out together, they want that even more than winning the lottery.

4. *It's about life.* People are not interested in meeting God to improve their understanding of the universe, or to reality test the theories of science, or to ascertain which charities deserve their financial contributions most. They want to meet God because their lives are lacking something. There is an emptiness, brokenness, or cancer in their souls that cannot be eradicated in any other way. And, by God! They want to *live*.

5. *It's about Christ.* Although they want to worship in spirit and truth, worship is anything but abstract. They want to meet God, greet God, embrace God, be embraced by God. They want to touch the marks of the nails in God's flesh, so to speak. They want to eat a meal together, see a tear in God's eye, and feel their flesh

tingle at the touch of God's breath. It's not abstraction they want. It's incarnation.

6. *Disciples seem to be the last people to get it.* Although it may be counterintuitive, the last people to understand worship in spirit and truth seem to be the disciples themselves. Established church leaders and members are very stressed over worship, worrying more about tactics (mountain worship or temple worship?) than the point of it all.

7. *Worship and mission are connected.* The one thing disciples seem to have the most difficulty understanding is that worship really is a function of God's mission. It's not a separate, sacred task. It grows out of a spiritual life; it results in a harvest of true believers. Worship attracts a seeker, grows a disciple, and sends a missionary.

There is a final element to the story. Whenever Jesus says things like "the time is coming, and now is" he conveys a sense of deadline. The time of waiting is over. The time to seize the moment has arrived. People have been coming to the well of Christian worship at any given church for a long time, but their numbers are decreasing. This may be because fewer and fewer people feel an urgent need to worship, but I doubt it. Meeting God is just too important to too many people. If fewer people are coming to the well, it means that the water is running out. Perhaps traditional church and traditional church worship are just not quenching the thirst of the public in the twenty-first century as they once did long ago.

CHAPTER ONE

Christian Worship: *Separating the Essential from the Tactical*

W hat is great worship? The very phrasing of the question suggests a shift from the Christendom world to the post-Christendom world. The question used to be: What is *good* worship? Today, however, good is not good enough.

"What is *good* worship?" is the question to be asked from a context in which Christian faith and church participation were the norms of society. The phrase *good worship* suggests a minimum standard of quality, a uniform process, or an archetypal form of worship to which all other worship can be compared and measured. More than this, the phrase *good worship* suggests that there are knowledgeable experts with the authority to distinguish between bad and good, and the skills to teach church leaders how to do it properly. That context has vanished. Such uniformity can no longer be expected. Those authorities no longer have credibility.

"What is *great* worship?" is the question to be asked from a context of cultural and religious diversity. Great worship is memorable worship. It is worship that has a lasting impact, and leaves a lingering taste in the mouths of spiritually hungry people. Great worship does not send people home to lunch or motivate them to serve on a committee. It sends people to the coffee shop to debrief and motivates them to join a mission team. Great worship is nontransferable from place to place, but is an original in every cultural context. It can't be standardized or packaged or measured against an abstract form. It is born from, and evaluated by, the spiritual lives of credible, local, indigenous leaders with whom ordinary seekers can actually dialogue.

Nowadays, among the decreasing numbers of people who attend Christian worship, you don't find people coming away from the sanctuary saying, "Gee, that was good worship! I love the fact that it is always the same, laden with abstract ideas, and reminds me of life in the past." If that is the tacit expectation of clergy and church musicians, not many people are highly motivated to attend. What you do hear from seekers and disciples who attend Christian worship today is this: "Outstanding! Awesome! That was *great* worship! It changed my life, my perspective, and my plans for the next week! I'm excited, moved, disturbed, challenged, eager to go deeper, leap farther, and climb higher!" People will return to *good* worship next week, provided nothing of importance comes up. People will return to *great* worship next week, no matter what comes up.

The difference between good worship and great worship is not that the former can be measured objectively while the latter must be measured subjectively. There are objectivity and subjectivity in both. Good worship is largely measured by personal tastes, preferred learning methodologies, and comfortable technologies; great worship is largely measured by personal needs, alternative learning methodologies, and multisensory technologies. Good worship is compared to a higher standard of historic practice, theological clarity, and community life; great worship is compared to a higher standard of visionary mission, christological clarity, and community service. Both good worship and great worship are very personal. Both are very community conscious. Yet they are very *different*.

There is nothing wrong with good worship. Worship that is orderly, uniform, standardized, predictable, and of high quality can be an anchor in an otherwise turbulent life. Everybody needs an anchor at some time. However, today nobody wants to be anchored all the time. Most people want to move with the spirit, and kayak the crosscurrents of daily living. They figure life is going to change, like it or not, and that worship had better help you paddle in the right direction. Whether we are anchored to the past or paddling into the unknown future, there are certain things about worship that remain constant.

The Foundation of Great Worship

The integrity of great worship lies in three fundamental assumptions. No matter what the worship experience is like, no matter what style or format it takes, and no matter how large or small the congregation, great worship is memorable and profound because of these characteristics.

The Intersection of the Infinite and the Finite

Great worship is a mystical experience. The infinite, nonrational, unmanageable, uncontrollable Holy intersects with our finite, rational, structured, orderly world to create a meaning we can never fully grasp, a joy that we can never fully communicate, and a significance to life that we can never fully achieve. We meet God; or God meets us. We are never quite sure if that meeting will simply give us a new insight, or whether it will sear our lips, dislocate our hips, and change our names.

While it may be said that God is always with us, and that every moment is an experience of grace, worship is a definite point in time and space when, with great intentionality, God and people connect. It is a moment to anticipate with hope or dread—it is a place to enter joyfully or fearfully. Worship is a peculiar meeting of humans, who think they know what they need, and God, who knows what humans really need—and sometimes those two things are compatible and sometimes those two things are diametrically opposed. The mystical moment may be one of comfort or discomfort, healing or fracturing, coaching or challenging, forgiving or judging, but always it is a moment of intense love. God's passionate self-sacrifice meets our passionate desire for reunion, and in the resulting explosion we are never the same again. And that apocalypse happens on a weekly basis.

Whatever else this mystical experience contains, it always ends in hope. No one should enter worship and exit in despair. No matter how comforting or challenging the experience might be, the possibility of new life remains tantalizingly before us. This hope may be experienced in the form of love, or it may be experienced in the form of *tough* love, but it is hope no less.

Worship, therefore, is a repeated experience of incarnation. It is the intersection of the infinite and the finite, in which God is fully among God's people. It makes perfect sense that the earliest church would shape worship around the Mass. The Sacrament of Communion is the very essence of worship, as God is fully human and fully divine, presented to people as their ultimate hope. It is a mystery and a paradox, but provides the sustenance for abundant life. The point is not that any *particular* liturgy must be performed in worship, or that any *particular* rite must be followed, but that Christ is incarnated in every experience of worship. Without Christ incarnate, worship is either mere superstition or a process of community socialization, both of which can be accomplished more efficiently by other means. Christ is the center of worship, because worship is the intersection of the infinite and the finite. Whether worship incorporates a *rite* of Eucharist, or simply holding hands in silent affection, it is all meaningless unless Christ is there.

Thanksgiving and Praise

The meeting between God and people may be prearranged by one party or the other, but there is never any doubt who initiates salvation. It is God's grace that stirred the heart or manipulated events to get you here—and it is God's grace that heals the heart or creates the person anew, and sends you out of here.

> In this the love of God was made manifest among us, that God sent his only Son into the world, so that we might live through him. In this is love, not that we loved God but that he loved us and sent his Son to be the expiation for our sins....We love, because he first loved us. (1 John 4:9-10, 19)

Therefore, the underlying theme of all worship is thanksgiving or praise. It is a confidence in God's grace. That is the reason the meeting between God and people takes place at all. Into the dialogue, we bring our requests, needs, hopes, dreams, questions, longings, failures, successes, and so on—and God brings gifts, answers, comforts, challenges, encouragements, and so on—but the climate of worship is one of gratitude. We can ask anything of God, but the one thing we need not ask God is that God should love us. That is already known. That has already been made clear. It is because that is clear, that we can ask anything of God.

Although the climate of worship is fundamentally one of thanksgiving and praise, it would be hasty to assume that there is any particular way to give thanks and praise. That this should be liturgical, classical, or stylized in any particular way is a matter of tactics. If anything, the prophet Amos sets us straight:

> I hate, I despise your festivals,
>   and I take no delight in your solemn assemblies.
> Even though you offer me your burnt offerings and grain
>   offerings,
>   I will not accept them;
> and the offerings of well-being of your fatted animals
>   I will not look upon.
> Take away from me the noise of your songs;
>   I will not listen to the melody of your harps.
> But let justice roll down like waters,
>   and righteousness like an everflowing stream.
> (Amos 5:21-24)

The point, obviously, is that the best way to give thanks to God is to do God's will, and the best way to praise God is to lead a godly life.

Spiritual Life

Great worship is part of an even greater spiritual life. It is not a stand-alone event for which people make time on Sunday morning, but that has little or no influence on the conduct of life and lifestyle during the week.

Great worship emerges from spiritual life. That is to say, it is not planned as the brainstorm of a handful of church officers, nor does it emerge from a computer program that selects the prayers for the day. It emerges from the serious, partnered, constant discipline of leaders as they read the Bible daily; pray for God's mission daily; personally participate in outreach; discuss spiritual matters seriously; mentor one another constantly; and generally align their lifestyle to pursue a biblical vision and *nothing else*. Good worship emerges from professional competency. *Great* worship emerges from truly deep and authentic spirituality.

Great worship accelerates the spiritual life. Part of what makes worship so great is that the participants know it has come out of the spiritual depths of the leaders; and part of what makes worship so great is that it then quickens the hearts of participants to seek God and do God's will. Those who are tired are energized; those who are burned out catch fire; those who are confused are focused; and those who are already running hard run faster. Good worship multiples programs. *Great* worship multiplies leaders of programs.

Great worship leads to deeper spiritual life. The spiritual life is a combination of discovery and calling. One not only discovers or receives spiritual gifts, but also discerns how God wants one to put those gifts into practice for the sake of mission. Worship is about linking God's mission to personal mission. It changes, redirects, and aims people at the mission target. Good worship connects one's time, talent, and money with the institutional program. *Great* worship connects all that you are, all that you have, and all that you might be with God's purpose.

These foundations of worship remain consistent no matter what kind of worship we do, or God does. If a church service somehow fails to be a mystical intersection between the infinite and finite; or fails to be an experience of grace and an opportunity for thanksgiving; or fails to spring from, and lead to, an authentic and deep spiritual life; then it is simply not worship. It may be a great choral performance or rock concert, or an edifying lecture, or a great dinner at the club, or a terrific fund-raiser or vote-getter for a philanthropic cause—but it isn't worship. Worship happens when the infinite and the finite intersect, joyful thanksgiving breaks out, and people devote themselves to a spiritual life.

The Function of Great Worship

The power of great worship lies in three basic organizational functions: worship as mission, as community, and as companionship with Christ. As a collective activity, worship is *useful*. It accomplishes something. It participates in a disciple-making and disciple-deploying process that is the wider work of the church. To speak of the function of worship is not to trivialize it. So long as the foundations of worship remain, worship retains it own integrity.

The reality is that worship has *always* had a functional dimension. Organizationally, traditional worship served to socialize newcomers into the neighborhood, explain institutional obligations and public policies to members, draw volunteers into offices and program leadership, and support pastoral care initiatives within the congregation. These are all organizational functions. One reason denominations keep statistics on worship attendance, confirmation, and participation in the sacraments is to track the success of this organizational function. If people don't come to worship, volunteerism and financial strength will decline. In the days of Christendom, good worship was actually more important than great worship, because good worship supported the organizational uniformity and program stability of the church. Too much great worship encouraged maverick behavior and disharmony.

That is why the functions of great worship need to be made very clear. There is no need for lapses of accountability or disharmony in worship. Once the foundations of great worship are protected, the functions of great worship can create as much loyalty and unity in the congregation of the future post-Christendom church as the functions of good worship created in the congregation of the past Christendom church.

Worship as Mission

The moment Jesus declared the Great Commission (Matt 28:18-20), and then reinforced it with his promise to send the Holy Spirit (Acts 1:7-8), the purpose of worship was forever changed. Although the story of the Acts of the Apostles is not explicitly about the transformation of temple and synagogue worship into worship designed for the Gentiles, the implication is clear. In a crucial turning point in Corinth, Paul becomes fed up with restrictive, dogmatic expectations about good worship, and literally goes next door to the home of Titius Justus to establish worship in a house church outside the approved institutional religious structure. His accusers say: "This man is persuading people to worship in ways contrary to the law" (Acts 18:13). God responds by reassuring Paul in a dream: "Speak . . . for I have many people in this city" (Acts 18:9 RSV).

The foundation of worship already links worship to the spiritual life, as worship springs from and leads toward authentic discipleship. Functionally, however, worship *is* a form of mission. It employs the indigenous cultural forms of any given microculture, in order to introduce seekers to Christ. Or, it employs whatever learning methodologies are most effective in any given microculture, in order to motivate disciples to witness, serve, and model authentic Christian faith.

Great worship is designed with a missional purpose. That purpose may be instruction, coaching, healing, cherishing, or celebration, separately or in combinations, but it is clearly aimed to achieve some result, or to open people to some avenue of grace. This does not mean that worship is any less an experience of divine grace, for all the intentionality of human preparation. No one would claim, for example, that all the choir rehearsals, liturgical crafting, and sermon preparation make good worship any less a divine experience of grace, either. It is just that worship is not intended by God or planning teams to send people to coffee, refreshments, and conversation with their friends. It is intended to help people drink deeply from the fountain of grace, and send them to bring living water to the rest of the world.

Worship as Community

Great worship actually builds and nurtures community. It is not just that worship is performed by a community, but that worship literally shapes community out of a crowd. The function of worship is to generate and maintain a spirit of unity and relationships of high trust. Great worship happens when the unison responses and covenant promises of worship are actually lived out in profound mutual support and high trust in the innovative missions of the church during the week.

Authentic community is not revealed through declared assent to public policies and theological dogmas on Sunday, and subsequent backbiting or layers of supervisory bureaucracy through the rest of the week. It is revealed when significant personal support happens between laity, regardless of dependence on professional pastoral care; and when effective mission is rapidly responsive to emerging community needs, regardless of dependence on board approvals. There is a continuity of mutual support and high trust that visibly transfers from worship to daily life.

Community for the body of Christ is really defined by the shared core values, convictions, vision, and mission of the people. I first described these in my book *Moving Off the Map* (Abingdon Press, 1998). Core values are positive, predictable behavior patterns; bedrock convictions are sources of faith to which people predictably turn for strength; motivating vision is the joyful song in the heart to which every program, budget, and staff person is aligned; and strategic mission is the heartburst focus that captures the imagination of the public and elicits total commitment from members. The clearer the consensus and ownership of the congregation around *these* things, the stronger the community becomes.

The function of great worship is to nurture and enhance that sense of community. Worship should regularly and constantly articulate this identity. It should reinforce the values, celebrate the convictions, cast the vision, and motivate the mission. Great worship does not lead people into a fog of speculation, or freeze people into a glacier of crystalline immobility. Fog may be comfortable, and glaciers may be beautiful, but great worship aspires to be clear in the midst of conversation with culture and mobile on the mission field.

Worship as Companionship with Christ

If the foundation of worship is incarnation, then surely the function of worship is to bond Christ and people together in a walking, talking, companionable journey through life. Such a relationship is certainly more complex, and more mysterious, than ordinary friendships—or even extraordinary friendships. Yet it is no accident that Jesus himself employs the metaphor of bridegroom and bride, or that the earliest church should interpret the Song of Songs as a metaphor of Christ's love for the church. This is a lifelong companionship, presumably with as much or more mentoring, sacrificing, sharing of confidences, risking dangers, and celebrating milestones as the best marriages.

Viewed in this light, worship is not an occasional feast, but the regular breakfast between two intimates who together plan their day, make decisions about their children, and divide responsibilities for work. Christ and the church are not good buddies, but intimate lovers who are willing to give their lives for one another, shape their lifestyles around each other, and hold hands together through thick and thin.

Great worship reinforces that kind of intimacy. It is not an easy intimacy. After all, how easy can it be to be married to God? It will be a relationship that is liable to be very demanding and often ambiguous. The bride of Christ must live up to nothing less than the fruits of the Spirit, and make decisions that impact the lives of many people for better or worse. Yet there is a joy in that companionship, a sense of feeling good and feeling right about that companionship. People do not choose to go to worship lightly. They *look forward* to worship. They *live in anticipation* of worship. They *yearn* for worship. It is time well spent with the Beloved.

Companionship, both in Bible times and in contemporary times, implies adaptability and mobility. When Ruth marries Boaz, she promises to go where he goes. When Paul meets Jesus, he finds himself traveling for the rest of his life. When a church exchanges wedding vows with Jesus, she promises to follow him wherever he goes. And make no mistake, Jesus is on the move. The challenge to the church is to keep up. Great worship reflects that sense of urgency. If worship is adaptive or experimental, it is not for the sake of culture, but for the sake of Jesus. Worship is adaptive because Jesus is adaptive. Worship is experimental because Jesus is experimental. One moment he's in Jerusalem, the next in Philippi, and the next in downtown Memphis. Will worship be different? Of course. Will companionship with Jesus be different? Of course not.

The marriage metaphor may not work well today, because our understanding of marriage is not the same as it was in ancient times when the metaphor seemed so profound. Today the husband may follow the wife at least half the time. That metaphor won't work to describe our companionship with Jesus, even though many an established modern church would prefer it that way. Jesus is not going to follow the church at least half the time. If the church decides to stay behind, postpone that mission trip, or avoid adapting worship to welcome some new microculture, Jesus is *not* going to say, "Yes, dear, that's nice," and go on reading the paper. No, the point of the ancient metaphor is that Jesus leads, and the church follows or gets left behind.

These functions of worship also remain constant no matter what kind of worship we do—or God does. Worship *will* drive people toward mission, build authentic community, and generate a specific companionship with Christ. If a church service drives people to maintenance, simply motivating them to pay their bills, perpetuate a heritage, and keep the doors open, then it is not worship. If a church service merely entrenches denominational polity, advocates public policy, and gains intellectual agreement about sound theology, then it is not worship. If a church service only builds great fellowship, nurtures harmony between pastor and parish, and rewards membership privileges, then it is not worship. Worship targets the people toward the mission field, aligns the programs with a vision, and stakes everything for the sheer joy of being with Christ.

The Form of Great Worship

The form of great worship is shaped by a single, pragmatic, preoccupation: relevance. Relevance is not accommodation. Accommodation is about ignoring contradictions, smoothing over diverse perspectives, extending and rewarding privileges, and preserving harmony at all costs. In short, accommodation is what much worship in established churches (liberal and conservative) already does—and has been doing for a very long time. Accommodation occurs:

- Whenever there is a contradiction between what we read from Scripture in worship, and how our members behave in public, and the preacher backs down
- Whenever there is a difference in perspective about mission, conviction, or strategic priorities, and the intercessory prayers turn inward
- Whenever Uncle Albert or Aunt Nellie is offended by the music most appreciated by a newcomer, and the music budget is disproportionately in favor of the longest standing members
- Whenever debate looms about liturgy, sanctuary floor plans, and refreshments following the service, and the congregation refers interminably to ad hoc committees

All this is accommodation. All this expects the diversity of the public—God's beloved people—to accommodate themselves to the aesthetic tastes, political perspectives, membership privileges, and circles of friendship of an institution.

Relevance is not accommodation. Relevance in worship connects the church with the real questions, issues, challenges, and sorrows of all God's people who are in desperate need of grace. Relevance means that the real target of worship is not the members, but the strangers. These strangers are not necessarily unknown to the members. They might be brothers, sisters, parents, children, friends, work associates, and neighbors, in addition to newly arrived immigrants, and heretofore nameless microcultures amid the general public. The point is that they are strangers to Christ, strangers to grace. The stranger, the seeker, or the mission is always the target.

Relevance to mission does not mean indifference to membership. It is just that membership has been redefined. It has nothing to do with institutional maintenance (the right to vote, or the obligation to manage committees). It has everything to do with discipleship (the covenant to go deep, or the commitment to reach out). Either worship directly welcomes and addresses the seeker, or worship nurtures, equips, and deploys disciples to welcome and address the seeker. It is increasingly difficult to combine these two forms of worship in a single worship experience. Introducing seekers to grace, and taking members deep into discipleship, require distinct strategies.

Relevance demands that, however worship is designed, it will be constrained by four boundaries:

- *Great worship will be biblical.* Scripture, Old and New Testament, will be the textual, historical, and existential reference point for great worship. Other texts, alternative histories, and the life experiences of other cultures engage Scripture and are engaged by Scripture, but Scripture is the essential counterpoint to the investigation of God, life, and purpose.
- *Great worship will be dialogical.* The form of worship will always be interactive and experiential. It will include the spoken and written word, but communicate on more levels than simply the spoken or written word. It will be dramatic. It will be image-rich. It will be personally involving. It will invite conversation before, during, and after the experience. It will get people thinking, feeling, and talking.
- *Great worship will be indigenous.* Whatever the forms of worship might be, those forms will be the lifestyles, learning methodologies, technologies, languages, symbol systems, and cultural forms in daily use, by real people, in the context of the actual mission field. God's grace does not require learning a foreign culture in order to be experienced. Worship encourages people to come as they are, grow as they need, and serve as they are called.
- *Great worship will be pragmatically planned.* The form of great worship is pragmatic. Design worship in any way that works. That is to say, design worship in any way possible that helps a specific group of people experience the grace of God, and become moti-

vated and equipped to follow Jesus. It will be biblical. It will invite and sustain dialogue. It will be indigenous and readily accessible. But beyond that, it will be whatever it will be. There are no blueprints, no imposed standardization, and no uniformity. Every worship experience, in every place and time, is customized for each particular demographic.

If the foundations and functions of worship remain constant, then the forms of worship can change and adapt with integrity. However, the modern experience of worship is often just the reverse. The *form* of worship is rigidly and uniformly maintained—but the functions of worship in a larger process of discipleship are ignored, and the foundations of worship are confused.

There are objections to this pragmatic approach to the forms of worship, and it is instructive to recognize and respond to them. The reality is that the standardization, professionalism, and formality of good worship are actually *easier* and *less demanding* than the pragmatism of great worship. Assuming that clergy and lay leadership have more than enough to do already (what with visitation, meetings, program development, judicatory responsibilities, special life cycle events, and other demands on time and energy), the less energy spent customizing every worship experience the better. Great worship is demanding because:

- *Great worship is too much work!* It requires a constant sensitivity to the changing nuances of cultures in any given zip code, a readiness to upgrade technologies and adapt tactics, and an evaluation process that is weekly rather than yearly. The answer is that clergy must reprioritize their time and laity must rethink their expectations of pastoral leadership. The disproportionate balance of attention given to members over strangers must be turned upside down. Pastors must now give a disproportionate amount of time and energy to strangers over members.
- *Great worship will make unrealistic demands on laity!* Clergy alone, or clergy and choir directors alone, can no longer sustain the growing number of options in worship. Gifted, called, and equipped teams of laity will be required to take over responsibility for more and more aspects of worship design and implementation. The answer is that continuing education budgets for laity must be raised, and volunteer teams will need to be trained

to a standard of excellence the church has not seen since the sixteenth and seventeenth centuries. The deeper issue is not that the laity must be matured and trained (a vision that goes far beyond Luther to the early monastic movement), but that the clergy must be willing to let go.

- *Great worship will raise unrealistic expectations for integrity!* Not only will clergy not lead by professionalism alone, but also laity will not follow by institutional duty alone. Clergy must model and apprentice; laity must be disciplined about spiritual growth and ready to be equipped. The answer is that congregations must become clearer and more assertive about shared values, beliefs, vision, and mission, and elevate adult faith formation to status once held by children and youth education.

The shift from good worship to great worship has revealed certain chronic, contemporary misconceptions. As the foundations and functions of worship become clear, and the forms of worship diversify, we now know what worship *is not*.

Worship is *not* an experience of information download. It is not now, nor was it ever intended to be, the single adult education moment in the life of most church members. It is not the occasion for professionals or denominations to lecture people on politically correct or dogmatically pure abstractions to which they should give intellectual assent. The era of long-winded sermons, wordy liturgies, and financial demands for top-down programming is coming to an end. Fewer and fewer people want to return to a classroom. More and more people want to be touched by the Holy, dialogue with mentors, and fulfill their destiny in God's mission.

Worship is *not* a process of socialization and assimilation. Governments and institutions have too long assumed that the role of the church was to assimilate newcomers into the melting pot of mainstream American culture, or into the acceptable norms of local citizenship. Worship is not a tool for harmonizing American culture. It is not a vehicle to build ownership for a distant heritage. It is not another method to inform and promote philanthropic service. It is not the Rotary Club at prayer, or a political party in meditation. Fewer and fewer people will contribute offerings to churches in order to accomplish work that can be performed more cheaply by social agencies. More and more people will tithe to a church that goes deeper to address the roots of evil and experience the power of grace than can be accomplished by any social agency.

Worship is *not* a preservation society for classic architecture and music. It is not a rationale to preserve heritage properties. It is not a venue to perform any particular music. It is not a legitimate career option to employ otherwise out-of-work musicians. It is not a strategy to refine the aesthetic tastes of children or the general public, or to preserve the arts in an industrial society. Fewer and fewer people want to shape their lives around a property or an aesthetic taste (of any kind). More and more people want to shape their lives around a biblical vision and bold mission (wherever they might lead).

The Power and Limitation of the Common Lectionary

A form of Christendom lectionary emerged in the fourth century C.E. as a means of following the emerging Christian year. For centuries it was intended to guide the *reading* of Scriptures during worship and to orient prayers for the Christian feasts. After the Great Schism between the Western and Eastern churches in 1054 C.E., both traditions developed ever more elaborate detail for the Christian year as they defended two diverging calendars, and as a consequence the lectionaries each developed for their Christendom worlds became more and more complex. The ecumenical fervor of the late nineteenth and twentieth centuries C.E. accelerated the acceptance of a Christendom lectionary among all churches. The rapprochement between Protestant and Roman Catholic churches (i.e., Western Christendom) brought acceptance of a shared Christendom lectionary that supported a uniform Christian year. The Christendom lectionary became a "common" lectionary.

It is important to understand, however, that the Common Lectionary was so named, not because it was recognized and regularly used by ordinary people, everywhere, on a daily basis. It was "common" because it was endorsed by all church authorities, in most places where the Western church had influence, on a weekly basis. Insofar as it could be said that the Western world itself was Christian, and that almost every person had some connection with a Christian church of some kind, the Common Lectionary became the basis of public worship. It was the worship, synchronized with a Christian year, and supported by a planned cycle for reading Scripture in

Sunday services, in which the vast majority of people participated. After all, we were all connected to the same church and "they'll know we are Christians by our love, by our love, yes, they'll know we are Christians by our love."

A major turning point happened in the late 1960s through the 1980s as the Common Lectionary was applied, not only to the reading of Scripture in Sunday worship, but to the planning of preaching as well. Preaching the Common Lectionary became normative training in Anglo-Catholic seminaries of all kinds. This represented a major shift in North America in particular. Churches that had more evangelistic worship models (revivals, gospel choruses, altar calls, etc.) reoriented themselves to a standardization of worship. To be sure, there are still many pastors who preach topically and many churches that worship evangelically, but even these perceive themselves to be exceptions to what is "normal." Church members have largely forgotten that what is considered normal only really emerged in the last one hundred years. Denominations across North America developed new guidelines and published new books of worship. The "Consultation on Common Texts" finally led to the endorsement of the Revised Common Lectionary by nineteen denominations in 1991. This is the form of the common Christendom lectionary as we know it today. It is the norm against which all innovations are compared and judged.

In the early twentieth century, there were good reasons to develop and promote a Common Lectionary:

- The North American frontier had been settled.
- Public education was raising the standard of living for the ordinary person.
- The middle class was expanding.
- Transportation systems were creating a mobile society.
- Communication systems were breaking down cultural barriers.
- The rise of secular society demanded a unified defense of orthodoxy by Christian leaders.

To be sure, there was plenty of room for evangelical action. These were aimed, however, at backsliders and unrepentant sinners *who still had childhood roots in the church*. It was not a pagan society. It was a Christian society—just not a very good one yet.

In such a context, a Common Lectionary and subsequent standardization of Christian preaching and worship were highly valuable. A new professional caste of clergy, specializing in preaching, teaching, and membership assimilation, could be trained and deployed with greater ease. This professional caste of clergy could then be resourced by denominational publishing houses producing preaching and worship aids organized in three-year cycles. That allowed the clergy to better manage their busy lives between preaching and worship preparation, pastoral care, and advocacy. It also set the agenda for seminary continuing education, and provided denominations with a new and objective means to evaluate the quality and effectiveness of clergy in congregational oversight.

There were even more advantages to the Common Lectionary. As the Sunday school movement was transformed after two world wars into family ministries for emerging baby boomers, the Common Lectionary provided the structure for Sunday school curriculums and fellowship events. Once again, publishing houses found new opportunities to resource the growing churches of the 1950s and early 1960s; seminaries found new curriculums to develop gender- and generational-based Christian education; denominations found new roles for program staff to develop and grow new neighborhood churches.

Properly administered, the Common Lectionary easily became the oil in the ecclesiastical machine. It lubricated all the parts—energized and unified all the congregational programs. It could—and it did—take many church members and leaders deeper into the Christian faith than ever before. It could—and it did—unite the general Christian public around common threads of Christian orthodoxy and ethical behavior. It could—and it did—pave the way for the profound moral challenge of the civil rights movement. In 1991, nineteen major denominations, representing the vast majority of North American Christians, endorsed the Revised Common Lectionary, just in time for the entire initiative to reach the limits of its relevance.

What happened? Why is it that just when the Revised Common Lectionary reached a pinnacle of denominational acceptance, the rank and file of church members and clergy are choosing with increasing frequency to ignore it? Suddenly, what is normative today in local churches across North America (and especially among those same nineteen denominations that endorsed the Revised Common Lectionary) is not the use of the Common Lectionary, but the divergence from the Common Lectionary.

Church growth in North America generally peaked around 1965.

Since that time, despite all the public claims and public relations posturing, the membership and financial strength of denominations of every brand name have been in plateau or decline. The median age of membership has been increasing; financial contributions to denominational funds have been stagnant or declining. Denominations are closing more churches than they are planting. Although financial contributions by church members to operating costs have kept pace with inflation, financial contributions by church members to *benevolences* have been stagnant since 1965. Seminary enrollments are generally down, and the majority of seminary graduates either do not go into parish ministry or drop out of parish ministry within five years of graduation. The once well-oiled ecclesiastical machine is seizing up.

So many books and articles have been written about the transition from the Christendom to the post-Christendom world that the evidence hardly bears repeating.

- The North American frontier has *returned*. Only it is not North American anymore, but global; it is not located in space, but on the Internet and in the souls of broken and empty human lives.
- Public education and confidence in the advance of science are waning. The middle class is threatened, and standards of living are declining again. Traditional family structures are fracturing, and divorce rates are climbing.
- The advances in transportation and communication have opened floodgates for mass migrations and crosscultural change.
- Secular society has been replaced by a bubbling cauldron of spirituality, in which Christianity is just a small potato. The Christian year has either been forgotten by the public, or absorbed and distorted by culture in ways that people can no longer even critique.

In that kind of environment, the conditions that made the Common Lectionary so valuable are no longer reliable. The general public is no longer a mix of Christians and Christian backsliders, but a mix of lapsed Christians and generations who have no familiarity with the church whatsoever, with a few Christians mixed in. The caste of professional clergy has lost so much credibility as to be less respected than lawyers and politicians. The world is changing so fast, and new microcultures are emerging in such diversity, that three-year cycles of preplanned worship and preaching cannot keep pace. Learning methodologies have shifted from print to image, and from curriculum to experience, rendering many publishing house resources and denominational programs obsolete.

All this is *not* to say that the church no longer has an urgent mission. It is to say that the mission field has changed, and that the mission strategies must change with it. These changes include:

- The caste of professional clergy is being replaced by teams of mission-driven amateurs and cross-disciplinary professionals.
- The practice of membership assimilation is being replaced by the process of making disciples.
- The program of gender- and generational-based education is being replaced by ministries of cross-generational and cross-cultural small groups and mentoring relationships.
- The predictable worship that once depended on well-planned liturgy and highly crafted preaching is being replaced by less predictable worship that depends on carefully crafted environments and the creative spontaneity of God.

It is this last point, in particular, that has imposed limits to the value of the Common Lectionary. The Common Lectionary was designed for an era of denominational cooperation and Christian uniformity; so that wherever the highly mobile Christian went to church he or she would feel *right at home*. For better or worse, the world has changed. Highly mobile seekers and disciples now seek a church that will help them *feel right* at home. Therein lies all the difference.

The great strengths of the Common Lectionary have also become its greatest weaknesses. That is the power and limitation of it.

Predictability

The wonderful thing about the Common Lectionary is that there are no real surprises from one Sunday worship to the next. True, the sermon may have nuances and insights that are original, but increasingly, even the anecdotes and children's stories have been borrowed from a book. The delightful thing is that we can read that book—either in advance to prepare us to understand the sermon, or afterwards in order to pursue deeper threads from the sermon. Worshipers always know where they are with the Common Lectionary. It provides a stability we need, a rock in the midst of unpredictable change, an oasis where we can always anticipate the shade being just right and the water being refreshing.

The limitation is that the Common Lectionary is not easily adaptable. It is not just that the preacher would have to spend more time discerning and researching the texts for Sunday worship, but that every variation from the predictable path interrupts the flow of Sunday school curriculums, large group studies, catechetical teaching, and congregational fellowship. Moreover, the very predictability of worship contradicts the very witness for the unpredictability of God for healing, prophecy, and apocalyptic change. People do not want to hear about it. They want to experience it.

Transferability

The wonderful thing about the Common Lectionary is that you can worship in a variety of places, in company with Christians from a variety of backgrounds and traditions, and have a foundation for dialogue. Clergy can converse together in the local ministerial conference about the same texts, the same research, and the same positive or negative reactions from their parishioners. Parishioners can meet together in study groups, service projects, and public events and share their reactions to a common collection of weekly spiritual data. The resources for pre- and post-study multiply exponentially. Mobile Christians who value institutional membership can, indeed, go church shopping for the best church, and compare apples to apples instead of apples to oranges in doing so.

The limitation is that the Common Lectionary is not easily customizable. Contextualization is more important to discovering meaning in life than generalization. People are paying attention to local identity, rather than institutional ideology. A new microculture is being born every few days in any given zip code—and people are moving in and among various affinity groups at the speed of light (or at least at the speed of the Internet or marketing strategy). The pattern of worship that empowers them this Sunday limits them the next. The worship option that feeds them this year starves them next year. People are not only church shopping, but also spirituality shopping. The context of their choice is not dictated by loyalty to a brand name, but by relevance to their life situation.

Uniformity

The wonderful thing about the Common Lectionary is that it really did create a sense of global Christianity. It reinforced the Christian year. Not only did Christians everywhere read the same texts, and focus on the same celebrations, for Christmas, Epiphany, Ash Wednesday, Lent, Holy Week, Easter, Pentecost, and Christ the King Sunday, but also they could confidently expect Christians were reading the same texts and praying the same prayers for World Communion Sunday and Week of Prayer for Christian Unity. There was a shared identity based in a common practice that was energizing and comforting.

The limitation is that the Common Lectionary cannot cope with the deeper disunities that are fracturing Christendom once again. Unity of liturgical practice and Bible study focus cannot stand up against contemporary quarrels over abortion and free choice, war and peace, sexual orientation, genetic engineering, and environmental change. Nor can uniformity of worship bind Christians together in the face of radical differences regarding the interpretation and authority of Scripture, the nature of the sacraments, or the priesthood of all believers. The Common Lectionary depended on a middle ground of reasonable theological orthodoxy that has now been eroded by the fundamentalist left and the fundamentalist right. Identity is not shaped by uniformity of practice or dogma, but is shaped by congregational consensus for uniquely shared values, beliefs, vision, and mission.

Authority

The wonderful thing about the Common Lectionary is that Christians always knew that the chosen texts in the three-year cycle, and the published commentaries and resources that supported them, were chosen and interpreted by credible scholars and church officers. Scriptures were not pulled out of a hat, so to speak, nor were they interpreted or resourced by shallow or biased individuals who were no more deserving of respect than the average pew sitter. There was an air of authority about the Common Lectionary, as if every Sunday the worshiper could confidently know that these scriptures, however difficult to understand, *must be important.*

The limitation is that the confidence in the authority of nameless, faceless scholars or church officers to understand our local situation sufficiently in order to tell us what scriptures are most relevant has eroded. It is not just that they don't understand our zip code. It is that scandals and hostility from the pagan media have made people skeptical about the spiritual depth, moral respectability, and breadth of knowledge that these nameless scholars and church officers are supposed to possess. It is better that a plan for preaching and worship be developed by people from our own midst, people who understand our local situation. It is better that the leaders who tell us what to read, and who guide us in interpreting what we read, are clearly known to be spiritually deep, morally deserving of respect, and broadly knowledgeable not just about the Bible, but also about fields of inquiry that are so relevant to our daily lives.

Orthodoxy

The wonderful thing about the Common Lectionary is that it tacitly defended the theological orthodoxy of the wider church, and that it used the *entire* Bible to do it. Strictly observed and properly used, the Common Lectionary led Christians into all the hidden corners of Scripture. Therefore, it allowed Christian preachers to expound systematically on all the details of Christian doctrine and traditional practice. Church leaders could explain the unique theological perspectives or biblical interpretations that defined any specific tradition, but they could do it against the background of a common, complex, but broadly accepted theological perspective. Of course, it was a *Western* orthodoxy rather than an *Eastern* orthodoxy, but since the Western church has had more influence in shaping developmentally advanced countries, and has had more missionary impact on developmentally disadvantaged countries, that was a minor matter. This orthodoxy provided a bulwark again the atheistic, materialistic secularism that emerged in the post-war twentieth century.

The limitation is that orthodox theology is less important than clearly relevant Christology in a post-Christendom world. Investigating the distant corners of the Bible is less crucial than discovering who Jesus really is and why he is important to any given microculture. The enemy is no longer atheistic, materialistic secularity. The contemporary context is a culture of many, many gods and competing spiritualities, in which materialism is truly and literally a form of pagan idolatry. If the Common Lectionary is perceived as a strategic plan for relevant preaching and worship, or as a delivery system for sound theology, then church members and leaders are becoming skeptical about the efficiency of the plan. Integrity remains a key priority. But a strategic plan that answers questions that culture is no longer asking seems to lack integrity rather than preserve integrity.

As the twenty-first century emerges, the rigorous standardization that was the strength of the Common Lectionary has become its very weakness. The point is not that the Common Lectionary is useless. Far from it! It has been revealed to be *limited*.

The truth is that relatively few churches are entirely committed to the use of the Common Lectionary. Most churches have already recognized its limitations, and have already been diverting from its rigorous and routine use. They have been diverting from the Common Lectionary, but they have yet to have much clarity about what they are moving *toward*. Diversions from the Common Lectionary may have been helpful, but they have also sent the congregational programs of education and nurture into some disarray. Ministry is less well integrated. Leaders are confused. Choirs, drama groups, image producers, lay liturgists, guest speakers, and visitors are unclear on what to expect. The more ad hoc worship planning becomes, the more burdensome worship preparation becomes in an already busy pastor's agenda, and the more vulnerable the pastor becomes to criticisms about personal agendas, dictatorship, and indifference to membership preferences.

From the beginning, the Common Lectionary developed as a *Christendom* strategy. It was "common" insofar that it was commonly endorsed by denominational authorities, for use among people who were already Christians in greater or lesser degree. What is needed today is a *post-Christendom* strategy. There needs to be a plan. There is no question about that. Spontaneous attempts through the 1980s and 1990s to wed contemporary music, indigenous art, emerging cultural forms, and changing personal experience to the old ABC cycles of the lectionary have been inadequate or failed utterly. The new plan has got to integrate Scripture reading and interpretation with the daily lives of ordinary people in diverse contexts, rather than with the weekly lives of professionals in what is fast becoming an elite minority. Here is the challenge. In addition to a Common Lectionary for an extraordinary people, we need to communicate crucial Christianity to ordinary people. Let's call it an "Uncommon Lectionary."

CHAPTER TWO

A Case Study of Your Church

The presentation of this alternative lectionary for seekers and disciples is interspersed with the transformational story of Old Trinity Church. This is not a case study of a specific church. It is a case study of a typical church story. It is a story that is probably very familiar to clergy and lay leaders of all established denominations in North America, Great Britain, Western Europe, Australia, and even parts of Asia and Africa where the outreach of nineteenth- and twentieth-century Western church missions established new congregations.

Although there are bound to be details that do not fit your situation, this is really a case study of your church. The point of the story is to describe the stresses and opportunities churches will experience as they use an alternative lectionary for seekers and disciples to build another track of worship. It is important to understand that clergy and laity have been trained for decades to design, implement, and evaluate a particular strategy of worship known as the Common Lectionary. They were not trained to design, implement, and evaluate anything else. The creation of an alternative lectionary for seekers and disciples is not going to happen overnight. It will require learning a new perspective on the purpose of worship, the acquisition of new skills, the formation of new partnerships for worship design and leadership, and the ability to use new criteria to evaluate success.

In the chapters that follow, the story of Old Trinity Church will be used as a vehicle for coaching the tips and tactics that will help leaders develop an alternative, disciplined plan to reach the postmodern and post-Christendom public. Here is the beginning of the story.

The Story of Old Trinity Church

Old Trinity Church is a 150-year-old urban church at the center of small, culturally diverse, and economically declining city. The structure actually looks bigger than it is. It only seats about 500 people (including balcony), but it is set on a hill to look like a cathedral. It has burned and been rebuilt on the same site twice in its history, most recently in 1960 when membership peaked at 1,500. Each time it was rebuilt, good stained glass windows were replaced by even better stained glass windows; excellent hardwood pews were replaced by even better hardwood and padded pews. A beautiful communion table and cross were replaced by an even more imposing communion table and cross. Good acoustics were replaced by even better acoustics enhanced by a great sound system. The organ, of course, is a classic. Students from the university music college regularly come to practice.

Many people ask why the church is named Old Trinity. The answer is that in 1935 the church launched an off-site Sunday school that was so successful that it later became a church plant named New Trinity Church. New Trinity Church closed in 1956 for many tragic reasons, first and foremost that they tried to be a clone of Old Trinity Church and fell victim to the changing demographics of their neighborhood. So today there is only Old Trinity Church, in contrast to many other Trinity Churches of various denominations across the city and suburbs. They are a part of the local history of the city, churches with heritage buildings, a missionary past, and congregations that drive downtown to worship.

Although the church has now declined to about 800 members and 250 regular worshipers (100 in the summer), Old Trinity is known as a vital congregation. It supports a variety of social service programs in the community, manages a child day care center, promotes an annual lecture series in theology, and keeps a modest Sunday school and youth ministry with about forty-five children and youth regularly participating (100 in summer during VBS).

Most important, it is known for good worship. It is packed for Christmas Eve (especially the late service) and Easter (especially the vigil). The church is known as a great teaching pulpit, and pastors have traditionally been recognized as good orators. The choir is outstanding. The liturgy is powerful. The Communion is fast. Worship lasts exactly one hour. Yet Old Trinity Church is not known as a stuffy church. It is friendly. When people pass the peace in worship, they really greet one another with affection. It is OK to wear casual clothes to worship. People will feel free to laugh during the children's story; applaud a particularly great choral presentation; leave and return (assisted by friendly ushers) if they have a bad cough.

Old Trinity has two worship services every Sunday morning. Both rely on the Common Lectionary. The day of the Christian year is marked in the bulletin; the Scriptures in cycle A, B, or C are printed in advance for the next Sunday. The psalm is responsive or choral. The Epistle and Old Testament lessons are read by laity. The gospel is read by the associate pastor. The 9:30 service is smaller, older, and a bit more formal because the full choir is not available and children do not generally participate. The 11:00 service is larger and more diverse generationally and culturally. The senior pastor preaches the same sermon in each service. The Sunday school leaves after the children's story in the later service, where they will use a curriculum integrated to the Christian year and the lectionary texts of the main service. The idea is that the parents and children will both focus on the same lessons, for the same moment of the Christian year, in their own ways, and will no doubt talk about it at home over lunch. The church once experimented with Sunday school between services, so that adults could more fully participate, but nobody would drive into the city and stay that long, the kids were bored sitting in the entire 11:00 service, and there were parking problems.

One year, during an annual denominational oversight visit, the congregation was surveyed to discover what it liked and disliked about the church. The response was very positive. The people really liked the worship services:

- *It's predictable.* They said, "We like the fact that there are no real surprises. We know where we are in the Christian year, and we know in advance what the Scriptures will be next Sunday. The choir can prepare appropriate anthems, we can anticipate singing appropriate hymns, and the teachers can prepare appropriate lessons."

- *It's transferable.* They said, "We really like the fact that we can visit our grandchildren clear across the country, go to their church, and experience pretty much the same thing. And when our families visit us, they feel right at home. When we moved here and looked for a church, we liked how this one did all the familiar things really, really well."

- *It's uniform.* They said, "It's reassuring to know that on any given Sunday Christians all around the world are reading what we're reading, worshiping pretty much like we are worshiping, focusing on similar themes and ideas. We like to think people in our city can put aside all of their differences and perspectives and lifestyles, and come here to just be Christian."

- *It's authoritative.* They said, "There are so many voices today. We like to know that our denomination endorses our church, that we are worshiping the way we are supposed to worship. It's important that our pastor has been trained to design and lead a good worship service, and that behind our pastor are professors and church leaders who can rightly interpret the Bible for us."

- *It's orthodox.* They said, "We don't want to be extreme. We don't want our worship to be bizarre or weird, nor do we want our worship to be frigid and meaningless. We want to know we are solidly in the middle of what the church has been all about for centuries. We want to praise God like our ancestors praised God, and preserve an important tradition in the midst of a world of change."

The survey also revealed some things the people did not like. They did not like Sunday school between worship services, for example. They did not like liturgical dance in the chancel area, or more than two options to receive Communion. They did not like musical backgrounds to the prayers. They really did not like being encouraged to sit up front.

Fundamentally, Old Trinity Church highly values the Common Lectionary. It is the key to an orderly, traditional, friendly, intellectually stimulating, well-managed worship experience that educates adults, nurtures children into adult ways, and assimilates newcomers into a historic tradition. Worship orients church members to the Christian year, from the First Sunday in Advent, through Lent and the Season of Pentecost, all the way to Christ the King Sunday in late

November. It will acknowledge Christian Family Sunday and Thanksgiving along the way, but lament Super Bowl Sunday, joke about Valentine's Day, and ignore the citywide multicultural celebration that attracts 100,000 participants every August.

Old Trinity Church has experimented with more contemporary styles of worship. They do not give these experiments an equal share of the worship and music budgets, but they are open to the possibilities. These experiments through the decades include:

• In the 1970s they experimented with an informal, coffeehouse style of worship. The music was folk, blues, or jazz. They celebrated worship in the darkened gymnasium on Friday nights, with dialogue preaching, adapting counterculture music to Christian purposes with varying success.

• In the 1980s they experimented with praise or celebration worship. The music was rhythm and blues and contemporary Christian. They celebrated worship in a brightly illuminated gymnasium on Saturday nights, with motivational preaching, adapting pop music to Christian purposes with varying success.

• In the 1990s they experimented with Taizé worship. The music was Celtic and meditative. They celebrated worship in the formal church parlor or the darkened chancel area of the sanctuary on Sunday nights, with brief pastoral meditations, adapting New Age music and chanting to Christian purposes with varying success.

None of these experiments survived, although a Taizé service lingers on Sunday evening for about twenty-five people led by the associate pastor. The coffeehouse worship was not very successful, and only drew about twenty to eighty people depending on how popular the local musical group was at the time. The celebration worship was too successful, drawing as many as 200 people at its peak, but the facility was cold and the acoustics terrible. The volunteers couldn't sustain their energy and weren't replaced as they burned out.

Yet the staff and board of Old Trinity Church were smart people. They realized that the real failure of the alternative contemporary worship services was the result of something deeper. For decades, the core identity of the congregation really was a Common Lectionary kind of church. They didn't really know how to do anything else, nor was the congregation willing to spend equal shares of money to develop anything else. No matter how informal or contemporary the service was:

- The pastor essentially shared the same message (based on the Common Lectionary) that he was going to preach on Sunday morning.
- The service still followed the Christian year in the orientation of prayers, songs, and readings.
- The format was still the same process of "Come to God—Hear God's Word—Respond in God's Service."
- The expectation was still the same hope that participants would become church members, use offering envelopes, serve committees, and eventually mature to the point that they would attend the "real" worship on Sunday morning.

No matter how they attempted alternative worship, the congregation still operated from Common Lectionary assumptions. They still wanted worship to be predictable, transferable, uniform, authoritative, and orthodox. So by the year 2000, the church decided to go with what they knew, investing their energy and hearts in quality, Common Lectionary worship on Sunday morning. Unfortunately, no matter how well they do it, their congregation is still declining.

The picture of Old Trinity Church would not be complete without looking at the context of their primary mission field. This mission field is defined by the average distance people in that community are willing to drive and shop. That mission field has been expanding dramatically since the middle 1960s and is now a driving distance of about sixty-five to seventy-five minutes. That, of course, is the finding of the US Census, and the congregation didn't believe it until they did their own survey of the congregation. Most people in the congregation may only drive thirty to thirty-five minutes to church, but they also drive much farther to commute to work or shop in their favorite stores. The demographic and lifestyle diversity of that radius is their primary mission field.

There is an enormous demographic diversity in that mission field. Different ages, incomes, family structures, housing, jobs, religions, and so on. There are over sixty lifestyle segments ranging from highly affluent traditional families, to desperately poor single mothers and street people. Every spirituality on earth is represented, and the shopping channel is selling jewelry named for astrological signs and the goddess with record profits. Between 33 percent and 40 percent of the public declares no religious affiliation, and most of the 60 percent to 67 percent that claim don't really mean it. Less than 10 percent of the public actually attends Christian worship on any given Sunday. The rest are at the mall, in the gym, working overtime, or at home sleeping.

When the leaders of Old Trinity Church study the demographics, they are very puzzled. On the one hand, they see that there is enormous opportunity for Christian outreach. Vast numbers of people are strangers to the church and hungry for grace. On the other hand, when demographers ask these people what they want from church worship, they invariably say they prefer "traditional" worship and music. That is exactly what the church offers, but there is no influx of new members.

Old Trinity Church sees that its membership does not even come close to paralleling the demographic and lifestyle diversity of the public in its primary mission field. The church also sees that the niche public that it attracts is becoming smaller and smaller, and being drawn from farther and farther away. Every new traffic light and every emerging traffic jam is going to persuade its long-distance church members to look elsewhere for a church.

Old Trinity Church also knows that the two primary ways people connect with church are through worship or through a mentoring relationship. Its social services will not draw people into the church. Its children's and youth ministries will not draw people into the church. Its lecture series on theology will not draw people into the church. People will be drawn to the church because of the worship, or because they have formed a trusting, mentoring relationship with a mature Christian disciple who will bring them to worship. Worship is not only what will attract people to church, but it is also a key component to equipping the disciples who will then go out and invite people to church.

If the old strategies aren't working—no matter how beloved by the current members—what will? And can Old Trinity Church implement new strategies without losing its veteran members?

CHAPTER THREE

The Uncommon Lectionary:
The Basic Strategy

T he Uncommon Lectionary is a plan. It provides the same opportunities to carefully design and implement a strategy of worship as does the Common Lectionary. The difference is that this is a decidedly missional plan. It is not designed to assimilate and educate members. It is designed to grow and multiply disciples. It is designed to connect with culture, not the Christian year. It is designed to connect God with strangers to grace. It is designed to integrate lifestyle and faith formation. And it is designed to transform members into apostles, sending them into mission that may, in turn, bring more seekers to worship. The Uncommon Lectionary is a growth strategy, rather than a consolidation strategy.

One of the reasons congregations have already diverged from rigorous application of the Common Lectionary is just this: They see the need to connect with other cultures, grow up church members who are not all that mature in the first place, and start to grow again as a congregation. It's not that church leaders primarily want large worship attendance—although, if that is one of the primary ways people experience grace, why wouldn't you want large worship attendance? It is about having more relevance to the community, more impact on society, and more joy in walking with Jesus on the road to mission. As we explore a different worship plan that the congregation can move toward, I assume that in fact many church leaders have already left the rigorous application of the Common Lectionary behind (or at least they are trying to). These initial insights and suggestions will help these leaders clarify where they are going, and understand why it may be so difficult. But let me assure you in advance that by the time we have finished explaining the two cycles of the Uncommon Lectionary you will believe it will all be worth it!

The Uncommon Lectionary is a two-year cycle. Each cycle is repeated each year, or in small churches, each cycle can be alternated every other year. And yes, the two cycles of the Uncommon Lectionary can be combined with a separate traditional cycle of the Common Lectionary for larger churches with more resources. What you cannot do is blend the two lectionaries, because they are based on different assumptions, use different planning and implementation tactics, achieve different results, and measure success in different ways.

	COMMON LECTIONARY	UNCOMMON LECTIONARY
Assumptions:	Reality of Christian Majority, Basic Bible & Theology Awareness	Reality of Christian Minority, Little Bible & Theology Awareness
Tactics:	Professional Authority, Task Groups Design & Lead Worship	Leadership Credibility, Cells/Teams Design & Lead Worship
Results:	Biblically Literate Members, Theologically Astute Christians	Biblically Conversant Disciples, Christologically Alive Apostles
Evaluation:	Membership Growth, Financial Support, Quality Programs, Harmonious Congregation	Spiritual Growth, Extensive Outreach, Personal and Team Mission, Changed World

Any lectionary is, after all, a tactic. It is only effective if it is based on accurate perceptions of community context and organizational mission; connected with a series of other tactics that support and enhance it; and if leaders choose the right ways to measure success and are diligent in doing so.

Changing the lectionary strategy is not like upgrading the hymnbook. That can be stressful enough! But in the end, the hymnbook can be replaced and worship will continue much as it did before. A lectionary is a pervasive strategy that connects all the components of worship, education, and nurture in a church. Change that, and you influence everything else. The tactics, anticipated results, and methods to measure success in everything else begin to change as well. If one of the greatest leverage points for change in the church is worship, then one of the greatest leverage points for changing worship is the lectionary strategy around which worship is developed.

The very fact that changing the hymnbook proves to be so stressful is revealing. It reveals the unspoken assumption that worship is at its best when it is predictable, familiar, and uniformly the same in all congregations of the same tribe. It is even more revealing that in order to change the hymnbook, all the resources of congregational and denominational hierarchical authority must reassure the church that the new hymnbook is even more orthodox than before, and that it will eventually promote even greater inclusiveness and harmony. All these are typical mind-sets of the Common Lectionary rooted, as it is, in Christendom. The hymnbook eventually changes. The mind-set not only remains, but has been reinforced. Worship attendance continues to decline. It is no accident that it took over forty years for the Common Lectionary to become the Revised Common Lectionary.

The Uncommon Lectionary also has a mind-set, but it is a different mind-set. Predictability, familiarity, and uniformity are less important than experience, relevance, and mission impact. Not only can the hymnbook be changed with little stress, but it will almost certainly be changed with some regularity. All the routines of worship are scrutinized with a different method of evaluation. Change will not require the authority of a professional hierarchy, but the credibility of spiritually growing adults organized into cells and teams. It will not be measured by the degree of satisfaction among members, but by the number of microcultures in the zip code that connect with worship. In a world of such fast-paced change and constant revolution, it should not take over forty years to revise the plan of worship. The Uncommon Lectionary is a two-year cycle. Each Sunday the single text or worship theme is large enough to be customized and applied to the changing context of the mission field. Cell groups or mission teams combining professionals and amateurs within or beyond the church undertake the process of customization and application. Their team reflection is informed, in turn, by other key scriptures. Worship emerges bottom-up instead of top-down—from the credibility of local leaders rather than the authority of unknown church officials. Worship grows outside-in rather than inside-out—from strangers to grace connecting with God, rather than from membership transfers and confirmations of youth who have been assimilated into the institution.

The Seeker Cycle introduces strangers to grace to the fifty-two basic biblical stories and passages that every Christian needs to know. It does not attempt to comprehensively cover the Bible. In a world in which people do not know the difference between an Old or a New Testament, this cycle addresses the twenty-six Old Testament Scriptures and the twenty-six New Testament Scriptures that are so fundamental to Christian faith and practice that every person who professes Christ ought to be familiar with them.

The Disciple Cycle takes seekers deeper into Christian faith, and personal and congregational mission. This cycle does lead people comprehensively through the entire Bible, but it does so by dividing the calendar year into five separate story lines that represent the overarching themes of Scripture from the perspective of Christian missionary tradition. This cycle focuses faith in God through the experience of Jesus Christ, and intentionally connects worship with midweek small groups.

The following chapters will take you deeper into the details of the two cycles of the Uncommon Lectionary. It must be said, however, and without any sense of judgment or condescension, that the cycles of the Uncommon Lectionary are as helpful to church members as to those who are alienated from the church. The fact is that many church members are as much strangers to grace as the general public. They often do not know the basic biblical stories and passages that every Christian should know. They often do not know the five story lines that make up salvation history. They may not participate in serious adult spiritual growth that results in personally fulfilling mission and outreach.

This may seem surprising, alarming, or even annoying to the proponents of the Common Lectionary. Certainly, the Common Lectionary was also designed to educate members in Scripture and take them deep into faith, and for a while it worked. The problem was that it assumed too much. It assumed a Christendom world, a basic familiarity with Christian terminology, and plenty of time for members to hang in there as experts designed and redesigned a circuitous route through all the corners of the Bible over three years. In the end, many pastors and church leaders discovered that there was so much training required to even position the congregation to use the Common Lectionary effectively that there was little time or energy to then actually do it. People first had to be educated to worship. Ironically, this made the Common Lectionary more labor intensive, and less of an experience of grace, than the theology behind the Common Lectionary actually advocated. So much teaching, training, memorization, repetition, and commentary study left people wondering, *Where's the grace?*

There is a fundamental shift in philosophy from the Common Lectionary to the Uncommon Lectionary. It is a different leadership mentality—and a different congregational expectation. Expectations must move:

- *From predictability to adaptability.* Although the Uncommon Lectionary is a plan, there is only one biblical story, passage, or text that is the preaching focus and theme of worship. This is not mere pericope of a few verses, but a block of text sometimes chapters long. Worship designers and leaders can focus on whatever elements of the passage seem most relevant to the public at the time.
- *From transferability to contextuality.* Although the cycles of the Uncommon Lectionary may be followed by many churches, the context is much more influential for the design of worship than the commentaries written by experts. Visit two churches, both following the Uncommon Lectionary, and there may be nothing recognizably the same. Worship will be designed specifically with the demographic and lifestyle profile of the primary mission field in mind, rather than generalizations about universal truth.

- *From uniformity to identity.* The Uncommon Lectionary follows a calendar, but it is not the calendar of the Christian year. It is the real calendar, the normal year that shapes the lives of ordinary people. There are times of spiritual significance for the real calendar, but they are not rooted in church history. Christians are brought into conversation with the pagan anniversaries of Valentine's Day, Mother's Day, Super Bowl Sunday, or the local fishing derby. What is important in that dialogue is not the exposition of Epiphany, but the clear declaration and modeling of the core values, beliefs, vision, and mission that are the consensus and driving force of the local congregation.

- *From authority to credibility.* The Uncommon Lectionary influences the lives of seekers and disciples through the credibility of the spiritual lives of the design and leadership teams that develop each worship service. This is not a matter of professionalism, but of authenticity. Worship reveals the heart, the spiritual depth, the life struggle, and spiritual victory of local leaders who form the teams of worship development. It is personal. It may occasionally seem "amateur." But people accept belief in the possibilities and accept the challenges of worship because they actually know the leaders who have realized the possibilities and suffered the consequences of faith.

- *From orthodoxy to Christology.* The Uncommon Lectionary neither embraces nor avoids extremes. It is not designed to present a systematic theology. It is designed to introduce people to Christ and explore what companionship with Jesus in life and mission is all about. The only question of burning importance in the post-Christendom world is the same as in the pre-Christendom world: *Who is Jesus—and why does he matter to my microculture?*

In the perspective of Christian history, the Uncommon Lectionary returns the church to the first millennium of its existence. This philosophical shift may be the hardest task for church leaders to accomplish, because we are so used to the Christendom of the second millennium of the church's existence, and we cannot figure out why the strategies we know so well aren't working into the third millennium of the church's existence. Once this shift in mind-set begins to happen, the purpose and tactics of the Uncommon Lectionary are actually quite simple and straightforward.

Before a church begins to launch the Seeker Cycle and Disciple Cycle of the Uncommon Lectionary, the pastor, staff, and church board need to address three key work areas. Doing so in advance will help ensure the new worship strategy can be developed successfully and with less stress.

Attitude Is Everything: The Number One Key to Transitioning Your Worship

The church exists for the mission of Christ. It does not exist for the privileges of members. That fundamental attitude shift will make any lectionary strategy work better, whether it is the Common Lectionary, the Uncommon Lectionary, or any future lectionary. Yet it must be said that the very assumptions of the Common Lectionary make this change in attitude harder. The atmosphere of predictability, familiarity, and uniformity—and the dependency on professional expertise—encourages an institutionalization of worship. It encourages an elitism, an in-group mentality, that discourages inclusivity. Most churches, of course, will be offended by that comment. They see themselves as welcoming and friendly. Yet the fact remains that the Common Lectionary has become so cumbersome to learn and maintain, and so difficult to interpret and make relevant, that newcomers wonder what world church members actually inhabit. And let's be honest! It is not just the newcomers who are wondering this. Veteran church members and their children are wondering, too!

It's not about membership! It's about God's mission! The member is less important than the stranger. The member exists to introduce strangers to God's grace. If members have not experienced God's grace, or are unwilling to help others experience God's grace, then they really shouldn't be a member. They may be welcomed as seekers. Indeed, they should be loved and cherished as seekers. But members reach out to strangers. That is their fundamental attitude.

Most churches implicitly or explicitly recognize this missional attitude in their membership or confirmation vows. This is not anything really new. The problem is that churches rarely hold members accountable for those vows. Church leaders are too worried about financial stability; too anxious to preserve corporate harmony; too guilty about confronting the hidden selfishness that is the original sin entrapping all people. Members are just as selfish as nonmembers, just as consumer oriented as nonmembers, and just as defensive about their personal tastes, opinions, and habits as nonmembers. The difference is that members should be willing to fight this inner selfishness. They should be willing to model a more radical generosity. They should be prepared to hold one another accountable to their membership vows. Membership is a commitment to participate in Christ's mission.

The same Christendom world that birthed the Common Lectionary also came to assume that the mission had generally been accomplished (at least in their country, state, and neighborhood). The mission is far away. They may pay for it, send missionaries to address it, and pray for it, but they are not really a part of it. So long as the mission is "way out there," membership is understood as a commitment to consolidating Christian resources and nurturing people who are already Christian. This is the real reason why, even in churches that do both traditional and contemporary worship services, over 80 percent of the worship budget goes to the traditional worship. The bottom-line attitude is that a contemporary service that is more accessible to the general public is not really necessary.

That attitude must change.

The way you change that attitude is by experiencing a *heartburst*. A *heartburst* is what Philip experienced for the Ethiopian businessman; what Peter experienced for the centurion Cornelius; what Paul experienced for the Macedonians in Philipi; what Celtic monks experienced for the Vikings; what Wesley experienced for the working class; what Mother Teresa experienced for the poor in Calcutta; or what the best church planters today experience for whatever microculture has emerged on the corner or in the food court. A heartburst is a sudden, powerful, divine, urgent, and compelling desire to help that particular stranger (or group of strangers) experience the grace that they need the most. And worship (that intersection of the infinite and the finite) is one of the best ways to do it.

It is certainly helpful for your staff and church board to begin a serious study of demographic diversity and lifestyle trends in your primary mission field, but study alone rarely generates a heartburst. Only dialogue and direct interaction will do that. Here are the steps that can change an attitude.

1. The people will not go where the pastor has not already gone. Therefore, the senior pastor must spend much more time with nonmembers, nonchurchgoers, and the 30 percent to 40 percent of the general public with no religious affiliation. Volunteer to be on-call as the chaplain to the Fire Department; connect with social service and health care agencies; or just go lurk in bars, malls, sports arenas, dangerous neighborhoods, and other places where respectable clergy rarely go. If it helps develop conversations with people you rarely talk to, then start riding a motorcycle, get a tattoo, or do whatever you can to avoid looking like clergy. And no, don't do it in the pulpit. It will only annoy your members and accomplish nothing. Just try to blend in, listen hard, and risk conversation.

2. Define your primary mission field. Calculate the average distance or average commuting time people in your community and in your church are willing to travel to work and shop. Then send the board members in automobiles to see how far they can get, by any means of transportation, using any highway or train track, in that time frame. Have them report in by cell phone. Draw a map of the mission field. Start learning about the diversity of the public in that primary mission field, and pray for them constantly.

3. Develop focus groups with demographic and lifestyle segments currently not represented, or underrepresented, in your congregational worship. Involve your staff and lay leaders, but especially your organist or choir director, choir members, ushers, greeters, and anyone else involved in worship preparation or leadership. Be sure to take guests to the best restaurants in town (not the second best). Pay for dinner out of your own pockets (not out of the operating budget of the church) in exchange for conversation about what it is like to live the way these strangers live.

4. Deploy as many "listening-prayer triads" as possible into the primary mission field. Triads covenant to meet once a week, over an extended period of time, to pray for strangers, read the Acts of the Apostles, and spend time lurking and listening in any public place. They debrief to discern the questions and needs of the public, and to pray for strangers. Finally, they give feedback to the staff and board about all that they are learning. I described

this strategy first in my book *Moving Off the Map*, but you can focus it here for worship change. Again, specifically involve your music and worship developers and leaders in the triads.

5. Watch for the tears and create conversations among members. The Holy Spirit works. As people begin to experience "bursting hearts" for individuals or groups beyond the church, draw them into conversation to broaden and focus your sense of mission. Begin to reflect on how worship could be changed, focused, or adapted to help them experience grace.

Heartbursts do not require consensus in order to change the corporate attitude of a church. All that is required is about 20 percent of the membership and the majority of staff and lay leaders. When that minority begins to experience a compelling desire to reach out to strangers in the name of Christ, you are ready to rethink your worship strategy.

Cells and Teams Are the Basic Units of Mission: The Number Two Key to Transitioning Your Worship

The traditional method of designing and leading worship (encouraged by the professionalism of the Common Lectionary) will not work for the seeker-sensitive and disciple-multiplying church. The traditional method is based on committees and professional associations.

1. A worship committee, elected for reasons of talent and interest, and usually representational of various groups within the church, sets broad policy about how all worship options will be done.
2. The staff, and specifically the senior pastor and organist/choir director, will design the liturgy, message, and music for any given Sunday with reference to the Christian year, traditional practices and beliefs of the denomination, and any special circumstances within the church.
3. The clergy will develop sermons and prayers from its library of expertise, and in personal or online conversation with lectionary discussion groups made up of professional peers.

The worship is then presented by talented and trained leaders, and appreciated (or enjoyed) by the members for their edification, inspiration, or comfort. Criticism of policy goes back to the worship committee; criticism of performance goes back to the staff; and criticism of message goes back to the pastor.

The new method of designing and leading worship involves a shift from task groups of talented, representative leaders to cell groups of passionate and called missionaries. I describe the basic principles of mission teams and cell groups in *Christian Chaos: Revolutionizing the Congregation* (Abingdon Press, 1999).

Teams are not task groups. Team members are not elected or representational, but handpicked by a mission-driven leader who embodies and focuses the heartburst of worship. Team members are chosen not only for talent, but for passion, calling, and a willingness to hold one another accountable for mission results in constant team evaluation. Teams do not require worship committees to oversee them. Teams are reasonably trusted by the church to function within clear boundaries of values, beliefs, vision, and mission.

Teams are not committees. They are cell groups. Teams meet together every week, not only to rehearse, brainstorm, or plan, but to pray extensively, to support one another in disciplined spiritual and personal growth, and to hold one another accountable for their Christian behavior in daily living.

Here is a basic structure of team deployment assumed by the Uncommon Lectionary:

1. A distinct design team is formed for every worship option in the church. The minimum team includes a message shaper, a music coordinator, and a process developer. In small and medium-sized churches, this may well be the pastor, the choir director or band leader, and the liturgist or worship leader. In larger churches, the team members may not be the same people as the actual worship leaders. The design team will grow or change according to the missional purpose of worship and the heartburst of the leaders.

   The pastor (message shaper) handpicks the team. They may be staff or volunteers. They meet weekly as a cell group to go deep into spiritual life and mission focus. They pray together, support each other, evaluate one another's lifestyles, and allow the worship design for any given Sunday to emerge from the spiritual growth as a team. They monitor demographic and lifestyle trends, evaluate the success of previous worship, consider new ideas and tactics, and adapt worship to make it more effective in outreach. The worship design that emerges is rooted in their spiritual growth as a team and their credibility in understanding the primary mission field.

2. Each member of the design team handpicks his or her own team to continue to shape the message, develop music, or develop the process or support systems for worship. They function as a cell group, and align their work to the overall structure of the design team. For example, a choir will meet to develop and rehearse music to align with the mission target of the message, but it will also meet as a cell group to pray for the strangers in need of grace, offer personal support to one another, and hold one another accountable to both a standard of excellence and a Christian lifestyle. Or for example, a technology team will meet to enhance the process of worship with images and interactive drama and to deepen the spiritual lives and sharpen the missional passion of the team members.

3. Additional teams will multiply as needed. These teams may be exclusive to a particular worship service, or span both the Seeker Cycle service, the Disciple Cycle service, and even traditional Common Lectionary services. They tend to be cell groups based around hospitality, personal support, and prayer. The same basic components for true cell groups are repeated. For example, ushers used to be deployed as task groups; now they are deployed as cell groups anchored in prayer, personal support, focused training, sensitivity to the heartburst of mission, and so on.

Again, there is no reason that teams and cells cannot be used to support worship organized around the Common Lectionary as well as the Uncommon Lectionary. This may not be the norm, since the task orientation and professional dependency of the Common Lectionary tend to militate against it. Yet it is certainly possible, and the more familiar a church is with true teams, the easier it will be to develop and deploy the Seeker Cycle and Disciple Cycle of the Uncommon Lectionary.

Reasonable Trust Encourages Adaptability: The Number Three Key to Transitioning Your Worship

The Uncommon Lectionary is designed to be adaptable, contextual, and more communicative of congregational identity than denominational generality. Although this sounds noble, it raises obvious questions of accountability. Worship, especially as it has been developed in the Christendom environment of professional oversight and membership privilege, is the single most volatile and potentially conflictive program of the church. If worship teams are going to adapt and customize worship that is sensitive to seekers and that grows disciples, how can the church be reasonably assured that quality and integrity will be maintained?

In the world of the Common Lectionary, accountability is assured by the rigorous policy enforcement of the worship committee, and by the expertise and oversight of the clergy. This is further enforced and enhanced by the oversight of denominations and the continuing education of the seminary so that good worship (i.e., proper, orderly, approved worship) is preserved. Pastors may well complain that they cannot attend all the distinct planning teams implied by the Uncommon Lectionary cycles, and church boards may well worry that independent worship teams may do things that somehow offend the members or compromise the theological integrity of the church.

Therefore, churches must develop an alternative method to build reasonable trust throughout the entire church in order to free mission teams of any kind to be rapidly responsive and relevant to the mission field without needless layers of management and supervision. I have written about this in several places (*Moving Off the Map*, *Growing Spiritual Redwoods*, and *Christian Chaos*). My summary here simply applies the same principles specifically to the transition of worship.

First, congregational staff and official board must build a clarity and consensus among themselves around the key elements of core values and bedrock beliefs. A *core value* is the positive, predictable choice they can expect any member of the church to make, spontaneously or daringly, in daily life. It is a positive, predictable behavior pattern. *Bedrock belief* is the set of deep faith convictions that leaders can reasonably expect every member will turn to for strength in times of confusion or stress. These are powerful, constant, habits of the heart that rescue people from despair and give them hope.

These core values and convictions represent boundaries beyond which no worship team can go. No matter how they adapt, customize, and apply worship tactics, no matter to whom that worship is addressed—and no matter what grace they hope strangers will experience—the worship will always model, teach, and celebrate these core values and convictions. The leaders of worship will reveal them in their behavior, message, and music. People will emerge from worship having learned and experienced many things, but these core values and convictions will be presented every time people worship together.

Second, congregational staff and official board must build clarity and consensus among themselves around the purpose and direction of the church. The purpose of the church is articulated as a motivating vision, a song in the heart, a rhythm or cadence to congregational life, that raises the self-esteem of members and makes them feel like nobility. It is the great purpose, the reason for being, of the congregation that extends beyond mere survival to some positive goal. The direction of the church is articulated as a strategic mission: few well-chosen words and a powerful image that captures the imagination of the public, elicits enormous self-sacrifice from members, and can be printed on the side of a bus.

This motivating vision and key mission represent the direction toward which all worship should go. Worship options do not take people in different directions, but use diverse means to take them in the same direction. The mission words and images are highlighted in every worship option. The song in the heart is sung, literally and figuratively, in every worship option. Complete strangers can meet by coincidence outside the church, talk excitedly about the worship that is so meaningful to them, and discover by the shared vision and mission that in fact they are members of the same church.

Third, once the staff and board have built a consensus around core values, beliefs, vision, and mission, then they must embed that clarity into every worship team. That means they teach it, mentor it, communicate it, and model it with the team leaders who in turn do the same with their team members. For example, the pastor models it to the design team; the design team members model it to their own teams; and so on. Then the staff and board insist on regular evaluation by the teams using the criteria of this consensus, and provide feedback loops to reveal if, intentionally or unintentionally, the worship teams have gone beyond the boundaries of values and convictions, or failed to align the worship experience toward the vision or the mission.

What is true for all groups and ministries of a church is especially important for worship design and leadership. Worship is just too central to the overall mission, and potentially controversial for congregational life. Accountability is not about defining and overseeing tasks. It is about embedding and monitoring boundaries. So long as worship teams remain within clearly agreed boundaries, they can then be trusted to adapt tactics as the mission field evolves.

The leader in all of this must be the senior pastor. Worship committees are too distant from the ministry and too slow to respond to the mission. If the Christian year was still normative in the lifestyle of the world, and if the world still changed at the speed of 1910, and if professional leadership only had to make sure that the Scriptures were correctly interpreted and the sacraments property celebrated . . . then a worship committee could manage well enough. But since lifestyles have changed, change itself has accelerated, and credibility is more important than control, the senior pastor must take the lead to cast the vision and set the boundaries.

Old Trinity Church

Old Trinity Church has had six senior pastors in the last fifty years. In that time, the tenure of the first two pastors lasted ten years and eighteen years respectively. The first pastor led the church through the rebuilding project after the fire of 1960 and retired exhausted and triumphant. His photo is still hanging above the fireplace in the formal parlor. The second pastor led this urban church through the civil rights era and founded many of the social service programs that continue today. If the first pastor was solid and steady, this pastor was quirky and creative. He initiated the coffeehouse worship alternative, which ended shortly after he left. Both pastors relied on the Common Lectionary, but over the later years the worship program and the outreach program drifted farther and farther apart. Worship did not motivate many volunteers into social service; social service programs did not draw many people into worship.

The third pastor arrived in the midst of growing consternation about church decline, and had a more evangelical vision. He added the third "Celebration" worship service that broke with the Common Lectionary and traditional style of worship. The "Praise Service" used contemporary music, but there was no particular plan for preaching, integrated Sunday school, or adult spiritual growth. The topical service proved very successful—too successful, in fact. Controversy escalated over the amount of time the pastor spent with new people, the integrity of the alternative worship experience, and the fact that the new service did not significantly grow membership, finances, or volunteerism for the social service programs. After about seven years of turmoil, the pastor left to plant a new church in the suburbs.

The fourth and fifth pastors each lasted about five years, and were among the most forgettable pastors Old Trinity Church ever had. One was to all intents and purposes an interim pastor whose main purpose was to bring healing to the congregation. No particularly strong vision was cast at all, veteran members were reconciled, the choir and the traditional worship services were strengthened, the organ was refurbished, and the congregation returned to rigorous pursuit of the Common Lectionary and the Christian year. About this time the Taizé service was begun. The other pastor was essentially administrative. He led the capital campaign that increased parking and modernized the Christian education wing, and helped restructure and streamline the board as a council of representative program leaders. He also began an aggressive policy to rent space to the community.

The staff configuration both evolved, and failed to evolve, in important ways during these fifty years:

- The first pastor, who presided over what are now known as the glory years, hired an associate primarily for Christian education and an organist/choir director skilled in classical hymnology. Both were highly committed to integrating the Christian year and Common Lectionary into the whole of church life.
- The second pastor, who presided over the activist years, hired an associate minister oriented to youth work and outreach. Although the organist retired, the new organist/choir director was very much like his predecessor, although even more performance oriented. Recitals and cantatas multiplied at high points of the Christian year. The folk musicians of the coffeehouse worship were never given much budget.
- The third pastor, who presided over the crazy years, hired an associate minister oriented to children and family ministries. The organist/choir director was too well established to change, but the band leader was elevated to more importance. This caused considerable friction between staff and their ministry constituencies.
- The fourth and fifth pastors kept the same organist/choir director, but shifted the associate minister to visitation and pastoral care. She remained throughout the tenure of both pastors.

Amid such changes, use of the Common Lectionary had shifted, but never been abandoned, over the years. At first it was an assumed method of operation running through all programs of the church. Then the lectionary texts were used, but very selectively, with preaching and curriculum stretching biblical applications according to more ideological purposes. Later, the Common Lectionary was honored as much in the exceptions to the plan as in the use of the plan. Old Trinity then reacted anxiously to reassert the use of the Common Lectionary, but this time it was less a strategy for spiritual growth, and more a strategy to assert control over the whims of the clergy.

John is now the sixth pastor of Old Trinity Church in fifty years. This is his third church. He has a reputation of being a solid and progressive leader and a great preacher. He immediately made key staff changes. He replaced the associate minister with someone who spoke Spanish fluently and could develop worship and outreach for the growing Hispanic community. He turned caring ministries over to volunteers. He kept the aging organist/choir director because the program was excellent and it would be politically disastrous to fire someone with longer tenure than any pastor in twenty years— but he added a salaried assistant choir director who hopefully could bring a more contemporary dimension to the music. And he added a half-time program administrator who could coordinate and grow social service ministries. John loves leading worship. He literally grew up with the Common Lectionary. People say he resembles the sainted pastor of the glory days fifty years ago.

John is now in his fifth year at Old Trinity Church, and his life is about to change.

Commentary

I interrupt this story to comment on the importance of this background information. In ancient times, a lectionary was a method to organize prayer and liturgy in accordance with the Christian year. Later it developed into a plan to organize preaching and Bible study into what became a three-year cycle of comprehensive Bible interpretation. Ultimately, however, a lectionary is not just a tactic for preaching, but a strategy to integrate all of church life into a single plan for Bible-based education, membership nurture, and community outreach. As such, a lectionary is as much a mind-set as it is a list of Scriptures.

This is why it is important to observe the evolution of a church over an extended period of time. Old Trinity Church did not actually begin

150 years ago as a lectionary-based institution. It began as a small church plant, by a microculture of immigrants for whom the experience of divine grace, a continuing relationship with Jesus, and an opportunity to praise God for untold numbers of blessings were of crucial importance. So they founded Trinity Church, which over time became increasingly institutionalized and historic to become Old Trinity Church. In the last fifty years, however, Old Trinity Church very intentionally became lectionary-based. That not only shaped its worship, it shaped its Christian education program and outreach strategy, its rebuilding and property renovation, its choice of technologies and learning methodologies, and its staff configuration.

This is a good thing. It is good for a church to become intentional about its life and mission. In the end, however, any lectionary is simply a tactic. If that tactic to integrate the life and mission of a church no longer works effectively, the founders and ancestors of Old Trinity Church knew what to do. Change the tactic. The question is, do the descendants of these ancestors in Old Trinity Church have the same spirit? Now let's return to the story of Old Trinity Church.

John is now in his fifth year, and his life is about to change. It will not change overnight, but it will change dramatically in the next three months.

John's first inkling that God is doing something to him that is unexpected happens in August. That is the month when John is blocking out his preaching and worship strategy for the coming program year. He is meeting with his choir directors, Christian education volunteers, ushers and hospitality teams, women's and men's group coordinators, and trustees. They review the Christian year, and are using cycle C of the Common Lectionary to anticipate what music will be performed, what concerts will be prepared, what curriculum adjustments will be made, and what sanctuary decorations will be prepared. John is beginning to block out several preaching series, make notes about key preaching points, and anticipate what social service ministries will be highlighted on specific occasions of the Christian year.

One day in August he returns home early. He sits in the kitchen silently brooding for a few minutes. Then he announces to his wife sadly, "I'm bored." At first his wife does not take him seriously. "Go play golf," she says. "Take a sabbatical week and meditate on the isle of Iona."

"You don't understand," he replies. "I'm really bored. I'm unfulfilled. I'm wasting precious time. I'm fifty-three years old, in the prime of my ministry, in a prestigious pulpit, amid people who generally like me, and the high point

of the coming year will be Handel's Messiah *on Easter, complete with sound and light show, and artificial angels descending on an invisible clothesline extended from the balcony to the altar. I don't think Saint Peter is going to rhapsodize on that if I happen to show up next June at the pearly gates!"*

Now John's wife starts worrying. If John starts doubting the importance of the Christian year, he'll start tinkering with the Common Lectionary. That may alter the patterns of predictable worship, alarm the longtime members, and eventually jeopardize their family financial security. From now on, she'll watch John like a hawk and help him through this midlife crisis.

John's second revelation came a few weeks later after a meeting with the worship committee to share and confirm the plans for the coming year. The meeting derailed when John announced his intention to limit baptisms to certain Sundays of the year, experiment with another method of distributing the elements of Communion, and read all four lectionary texts every Sunday (not just three). All these ideas were recommended by scholars and church officers in the latest commentary on the Common Lectionary, and all were bitterly resisted by the committee.

"Baptizing infants at the convenience of busy families is a privilege of membership," they said. "We should do Communion the way we always have done it, namely, the way we did it in the glory days. And we shouldn't experiment too much because Jesus always said, 'A bird in hand is worth two in the bush.' "

Suddenly John realized that the worship committee used the lectionary as a means to control change, rather than as a means to take adults deeper into Christian faith. He hastily checked the records, and discovered that after fifty years of using the Common Lectionary, participation in adult Sunday school has actually dropped from a record high of 40 percent in 1960 to less than 4 percent now. His own worship committee did not even know what Jesus did or did not really say, and were setting policy about how people could or could not experience God's grace. Meanwhile, the worship committee began to worry that John was becoming dangerously innovative. From now on, they'll watch John like a hawk and help him through this midcareer crisis.

John's third revelation came in September. Chafing under the realization that his adult members were not nearly as deep in their faith as he hoped or they had assumed, he launched a survey of church dropouts and marginal members. He had always been bothered that worship and outreach never seemed to connect. People who attended worship were not any more prone to volunteer for social service ministries; volunteers in social service ministries were not any more motivated to attend worship regularly. He sought out a friend and parishioner who clearly seemed to be backing away from worship attendance. Why?

"John," his friend said, "life is really busy. I've had to simplify and prioritize my life. My counselor helped me list the top necessities I need to address. They include my marriage, my children, my career, my volunteer work at the hospital and homeless shelter, my health, my intimate friends, and my aging parents. I can only do eight necessary things every week. Attendance at worship ranks thirteenth." John left wondering: How can our worship be so excellent—and so irrelevant—at the same time?

Finally, John had a heartburst in October. It wasn't a heart attack, although in a sense it felt like one. It was a heartburst. He was taking the streetcar back to the office after a denominational meeting, when an object suddenly fell onto the street bringing the streetcar to a sudden stop. Everybody hastily got out; the police and fire department roared in; a crowd gathered. A middle-aged businessman in a three-piece suit had jumped from eight stories up to die on the pavement at his feet.

"Extraordinary," he said to a fireman nearby.

"Not really," the fireman replied. "Jumpers are rare, since most modern buildings have sealed windows. But suicides are up almost 30 percent in the last fifty years in this city."

John found himself sitting on the curb being consoled by an unknown fireman. John was crying and crying and crying. "Fifty years," he kept saying to himself. "My church has been preaching the lectionary for fifty years. And the suicide rate has gone up 30 percent." Suddenly, his heart burst. It burst for ordinary, working class, businessmen and women, who filled the offices and stores and entertainment centers of the city around the church. Thousands of them, and their families, too, getting more and more desperate all the time. Hungry, broken, anxious, empty, and contemplating suicide. Somehow he had to reach these strangers to grace.

Commentary

Transitioning to the Uncommon Lectionary requires a significant attitude shift on the part of most users of the Common Lectionary. This does not mean that the Common Lectionary should be abandoned, but only that the mind-set behind its use is different. Moreover, unless the senior pastor leads or at least participates in this shift of attitude, the transition will probably never happen.

Most pastors never intend to lead an institution. The passion and power of their original calling are to mission and outreach. They may get sidetracked in many ways, but the Holy Spirit has a way of making them restless to return to the original passion of the call. First, the illusions are stripped away. The appearance of success is reality-tested against actual mission results in the world. Pastors begin to see the church—and the worship of the church—the way it really is. This reality is different from the theoretical perspective of seminary professors, or the institutional agendas of denominational officers, or the sentimentality of longtime members. Pastors begin to see behind their own illusions about their personal significance as preachers or their personal presence as leaders. It is easy for pastors to become cynical or bitter. Some will drop out or change careers. Yet once the illusions have been stripped away, the Spirit will seize them once again with the call to mission. They rediscover the authenticity of their spiritual lives. They are willing to take risks to make the church, and church worship, more effective to change lives and multiply disciples.

The one thing that is missing from John's story at Old Trinity Church is a pilgrim band. Most clergy cannot shift their attitude so profoundly unless they are part of a small, mutually mentoring group of colleagues. This is not a lectionary study group, although it can grow out of a lectionary study group. In John's experience, the Holy Spirit provided a mentor in the guise of a stranger, a fireman. John needed someone to help him give birth to a heartburst; someone to be a catalyst for his tears; someone who could focus his yearning for outreach and mission.

John returned home with a different attitude. He was not sure what to do, but only that what he had been doing was not enough. He was prepared to change worship, but did not know in what direction. He was ready to diverge from the Common Lectionary, but was unclear exactly what kind of plan needed to be developed.

The first thing he did was talk to his wife and family. Fortunately, they had always shared his deeper sense of mission, and supported him in this redirection of ministry. His wife wisely advised him not to decry or phase out worship based on the Common Lectionary, because clearly that remained a powerful vehicle for worship and spiritual growth for some people. And John would need not only the support of those people, but also the active assistance of those people, if he was to build another alternative to reach seekers and grow disciples.

The second thing he did was talk to his staff, including the secretary and custodian. He wanted to share his heartburst, refocus his primary team around mission beyond the membership, and enlist their active help to rethink the lectionary plan that would integrate church programs. He also knew that there would be stress ahead, and the first people to feel it and report it would be the church secretary and custodian. He didn't want to surprise them, and he wanted to make sure they supported him in conversations with the membership.

The conversation with staff had mixed results. The associate minister understood right away, because her experience with the Common Lectionary, traditional worship, and classical hymnology were making her impatient with the influence of Western European culture on mission anyway. The custodian only asked for personal support as he anticipated some inevitable conflicts with the trustees about renovating or decorating worship space. The secretary was clearly dubious, because she liked things tidy and predictable, was unsure how this would impact her workload, and suspected the treasurer (with whom she worked closely) would freak out.

The most obvious challenge lay with the organist/choir director and his assistant. John was reminded of Jesus' parable about the farmer with two sons—one said he would and didn't; the other said he wouldn't and did (Matt 22:28-30). The principal organist/choir director declared all his support with enthusiasm, but the senior pastor predicted he would do everything possible to block any departure from rigorous application of the Common Lectionary and Christian year. His assistant had lots of questions and doubts, but the senior pastor predicted he would fall into line eventually. And that is exactly what happened.

The worship committee was already on the alert for deviant behavior by the senior pastor, and leapt to the conclusion that the church was returning to the chaotic 1980s when the church attempted a "Celebration" service that was exciting and attractive to newcomers, but ad hoc, poorly planned, constantly controversial, and exhausting to volunteers. Their stress peaked when John said, "Just trust me." Trust was not their strong suit. Supervision was their strong suit. They did not like the idea that they would lose veto power over tactics in worship and be limited to developing policy about weddings, special worship occasions like the church anniversary, and the use of the sanctuary for funerals. John assured them he sincerely did not want to return to the chaotic 1980s or do simplistic praise choruses either, but he made a mental note that something would have to be done to deserve their trust.

Finally, John met with all the various music, drama, and support groups that helped design and lead worship, from the greeters to the choirs. Naturally, everyone wondered what the new plan would be.

"If we're not using the Common Lectionary, following the Christian year, or diversifying worship simply by the time of the service, exactly what is the plan?" John was only sure of a few elements of the plan. The plan had to be aggressively seeker sensitive. It had to really take adults deeper into faith. There had to be at least an annual strategy that was biblically based. It had to be open to constant evaluation and experimentation. And it still had to leave room for a Common Lectionary, traditional worship alternative.

John was very proud about how his worship groups responded. They were all anxious (especially the senior choir), but they were all sincerely ready to try. The Holy Spirit had been working in their hearts. They knew worship was crucial. They knew their strategy for worship was not really working. And they all wanted to fill the sanctuary with joyful hearts, take worshipers deep into spiritual life, and send disciples out to really change their city in the name of Christ.

Commentary

In the months that followed, John continued to explain and interpret his heartburst to any and all members and leaders of the church. He made no change in worship patterns yet. He did not diverge too much from the Common Lectionary, but he did reverse himself from his thinking last August. Instead of insisting that all four lectionary texts be read in every service, he went to the other extreme and addressed only one of the lectionary texts in worship every Sunday. Many people said the worship had changed, but it was really not the worship that had changed at all. It was John who had changed—and his associate minister and liturgists and even the ushers and greeters. It was as if they were in training for something yet to come. Meanwhile, John and his staff were designing a new plan for welcoming seekers and growing disciples.

John made two big mistakes.

His first mistake was to simply accept the existing worship groups and committees as the teams that could lead the transition to a new plan of worship. By raising expectations for creativity and innovation, he had also raised the bar for spiritual growth and personal support. He simply assumed that his groups, choirs, and committees would automatically become mission teams—and he was gravely disappointed. While some small group participants rejoiced in the expectation for disciplined prayer, Bible study, personal storytelling and support, intercessory prayer for strangers, and tithing to be part of the group, others resented or feared it. Moreover, some of the group leaders could not adjust from leading a task group and running a business meeting, to leading a mission team and running a cell group. John had failed to build in a training module for the group leaders, and to establish a time limit for group members to adjust.

The result was that it proved more stressful and disruptive to replace leaders and members in the groups and committees who could not, or would not, make the adjustment. He couldn't wait for an entire year to replace them, and he couldn't wait for elected officers to complete their three-year terms. So between personal persuasion and extraordinary meetings of the board to restructure some groups and committees, a lot of time and energy was wasted. Training also required more attention by himself and the associate minister than expected, and their own incompetence unfortunately was revealed. So they took a whole group of leaders to an event to help train them in teamwork and cell group life.

John's second mistake was that he avoided confronting the senior organist/choir director about his lack of openness to an alternative plan for worship. There were two fundamental issues that needed to be straightened out earlier, rather than later.

- The first issue was that worship was about Christian mission, not about public performance or the preservation of good music. And the mission was not to protect the aesthetic comfort zones of veteran church members, but to help all people experience God and become disciples of Jesus. This staff member was having a very hard time understanding that applause was not conversion, and that making an offering in the plate was not the same as discipleship. In his heart of hearts, he was not a missionary. He was a musician. And in many subtle and profound ways, that was communicating contradictory signals to the congregation.
- The second issue was about control. The organist/choir director believed that the Common Lectionary (and all that entailed about congregational life, education, and outreach) should not have alternatives. Everyone, everything, and every program should revolve around that traditional worship. He did not want to surrender any power over alternative worship services, and the bands, musicians, and liturgists they might include. His sense of

threat to his influence was actually very astute. A lectionary is the integrating force that coordinates the life of a church—and his preferred lectionary was in danger of being replaced.

By delaying this confrontation, John had actually prolonged and deepened the stress of change. The organist/choir director was able to vocalize his objections repeatedly, undermine the confidence of the senior choir, frighten longstanding members that the chaotic 1980s were returning, and intimidate newcomers who might have talents to offer alternative forms of worship.

Just at the point when John realized confrontation had been postponed too long, the organist/choir director resigned and retired. He had had a long, long tenure, and wisely decided it was time to leave. The church had a huge celebration party, and accepted the resignation quickly. John did not leap to announce his replacement, and vowed to personally be involved in future interviews. It was not taken for granted that the assistant would succeed to the shoes of the master. John wanted to do more mentoring to make sure of the choice.

Meanwhile, John continued to work on the worship committee. He and the staff and the board developed a set of core values, beliefs, vision, and mission that convinced the committee that they had good reason to trust John and the emerging worship teams. As the Seeker Cycle and Disciple Cycle began to take form, the committee had a chance to critique and comment on the selection of Scriptures. The exercise did more to reveal to the committee the limitations of their own Bible knowledge than contribute to the lectionary. It gave John more opportunity to teach his own worship committee, and help them see the mission story implicit in all of Scripture.

CHAPTER FOUR

The Seeker Cycle

The Seeker Cycle is modeled after the evangelical experience of the ancient mission to the Gentiles. That mission specifically addressed an amorphous, but identifiable demographic of the ancient world known as "God-fearers." Some of these people were pagans with a clear interest in Judaism and the God of Abraham and Sarah. Some were institutional refugees from any number of cults, temples, and religions that abounded in the ancient world, but that were no longer meaningful for increasing numbers of adherents. Most, however, were people deeply concerned about infinite meaning and ultimate purpose, and who believed in some unknown God. This was not a matter of intellectual curiosity, but of urgent need. They longed for real hope in a world of slavery, insecurity, and death.

I described these people in my book *Kicking Habits* as the "spiritually yearning, institutionally alienated public." Since then, the term has been shortened to the *SYiA Generation*. This is the fastest growing demographic in North America (and, indeed, Australia, Great Britain, Europe, and around the world today). They politely and indifferently acknowledge the institutional church, and brush it off. "See ya," they say. "See ya around, see ya later, see ya when I need an official ceremony performed, see ya when I need my passport signed, see ya when I need a food voucher, see ya when hell freezes over." Yet as they brush off institutional religion, they immediately read self-help books, check their horoscope, explore alternative spiritualities, and sacrifice to whatever "ultimate concern" captures their attention and promises a better life. They are often cynical, selfish, flighty, and foolish—and they are pushing up the addiction and suicide rate in every community. It is this kind of preaching cycle that Paul demonstrates briefly in Athens. He goes to the people in the agora at the time of day they are most likely to gather to shop, work, or talk. He does not expect the people to come to him in their spare time. He connects with their spiritual hunger by observing, and praising, their spiritual search for the "unknown God." He then introduces them to the basic story of Jesus Christ, interpreting that experience both from their acquaintance with Jewish history and their own contemporary literature. He does not try to unpack every doctrinal nuance of an obscure verse. He does not apply higher critical method to reveal the sociopolitical-economic significance of Scripture. He does not use the Bible to critique Greek culture. He simple tells the story or stories that any true seeker should know, and orients it all to Jesus. Nor does Paul invite everybody back to Sunday school. One can imagine that he has already deployed Timothy, Luke, Priscilla, Aquila, and Onesimus out into the crowd to mentor individuals and groups, answer questions, and build relationships.

The Seeker Cycle is a one-year cycle that introduces seekers to the fifty-two stories, passages, or extended texts that every Christian should know. The cycle itself is somewhat more complicated to plan and present, and I will explain that shortly, but the point of the Seeker Cycle is to connect with seekers, on their own cultural turf, in the midst of their own life struggles, using the learning methodologies with which they are most familiar, in order to explain who Jesus is and why Jesus is important to their microculture.

Who, exactly, is a seeker? A seeker is any person who is a stranger to grace, and specifically, the graces revealed and experienced in a relationship with Jesus Christ. Defined in this way, many church members qualify as seekers. They do not know the fifty-two passages of the Bible that every Christian should know. They have not experienced, but yearn to experience, God's grace in any number of ways. They have an abstract knowledge about, but no real relationship with, Jesus the Christ. It is vital to understand, however, that the Seeker Cycle is not primarily aimed at church members. It is aimed at people who are spiritually yearning, but alienated from institutional religion in general. The cultural norms, learning methodologies, and lifestyle habits of church members are not the milieu for the design and leadership of worship. You have to go out to the public, understand *their* cultural norms, learning methodologies, and lifestyle habits, and design worship *for them.*

The Spiritual Calendar of the Public

The Seeker Cycle is built around the *real* annual calendar of the public. It is not built around the *presumed* calendar year of Christendom. The year does not begin with Advent. It begins when everybody else begins their year, on January 1. The preaching cycle is designed to intentionally observe, honor, and dialogue with the key spiritual moments of the general public. These are their "holy days." It is only in respectful recognition of their "holy days" that Christians present, explain, and give away freely and without cost, the person and significance of Jesus Christ.

Consider, for a moment, the evolution of the greeting card industry. Greeting cards were the brainstorm of some entrepreneur who realized there was a market in providing words and images to tongue-tied, shy, or inarticulate people to share their love on important occasions. In 1950, those important occasions were basically limited to Christmas and birthdays, with the addition of cards designed around the Christendom year (Easter cards, Baptism cards, First Communion cards, Marriage Anniversary cards, and so on). By 2000, the greeting card industry had exploded. Not only do people seem to be even more tongue-tied, shy, or inarticulate than ever about sharing their feelings, but the number of important occasions has multiplied exponentially.

We all know that the English word *holiday* is derived from the ancient and medieval observance of holy days. These were days when people took time off from work and routine, for festivals, feasts, fun, and sacrifice to the gods. With the emergence of the secular world, holy days became holidays and lost their spiritual significance. However, with the demise of the secular world, and the reemergence of the spiritually yearning, institutionally alienated public (sometimes described as a new "pagan" world), holidays have once again gained spiritual significance. They really are holy days. They have a sacred character. They are moments in the calendar year when people connect with a meaning that transcends their own lives, participate in something that is bigger than themselves and that gives life a sense of structure, purpose, or destiny.

It may be that some days in the *real* calendar seem more obviously spiritual than others (at least to Christians). Passover is holy. Ramadan is holy.

Yes, Christmas Eve and Easter (with variable influence in different parts of the country) are holy. Further investigation of modern culture reveals the spiritual significance of Thanksgiving and Mother's Day. Keep exploring how people today find meaning and purpose in life around sports, entertainment, and nature, and we begin to see that "holy days" include Super Bowl Sunday, the NBA play-offs, Australian Rules Football (in Australia), entertainment awards nights, Earth Day, and on and on. The chart for the Seeker Cycle describes the spiritual calendar of the public in the far right-hand column (see appendix A). It is only intended as a beginning, because the calendar must be customized according to the country, region, city, or even neighborhood in which you live. For example:

- In Canadian cities there will almost always be some celebration of cross-cultural life (complete with food, festival, and music) in July or August.
- In Great Britain Halloween will be replaced by Guy Fawkes Day.
- In Germany, the public across the entire country will celebrate the collapse of the Berlin Wall.
- In China, Cuba, and other Communist countries there will always be celebration for May Day.

Local celebrations will be equally significant spiritual moments in the calendar year. The annual fishing derby, anniversary of the founding of the community, and other occasions will be included in the preaching schedule.

The point is that from a sociological, anthropological, and spiritual perspective, these events are not just holidays. They are holy days in a contemporary world that is a bubbling cauldron of spirituality, superstition, search for meaning, and quest for hope. People look forward to these days, plan their lives around these days, tell stories about these days, and preserve images and memories about these days. They buy greeting cards about these days. The greeting cards may be funny or serious, sentimental or profound, but they all reveal these days are moments of significance for the life and lifestyle of the community. When was the last time you heard somebody tell memorable stories of the last five observances of Epiphany or Pentecost in the local coffee shop?

.In order to use the Seeker Cycle effectively, the first thing your worship design team must do is revise and complete the spiritual calendar of the public *in your particular mission field.* Obviously, this will vary from country to country, city to city, region to region, and even neighborhood to neighborhood. Only you can complete it. You can only complete it if you research your mission field, and dialogue intentionally and repeatedly with the many microcultures in your mission field. After all, the spiritual calendar of the public will change over time. New cultural groups will move in or out; new generations will focus on different "holy times"; world events will decisively influence the memory and hope of the public.

Your team must uncover the spiritual rhythm of life in your zip code—in your primary mission field. You must uncover the issues, questions, challenges, hopes, patterns of meaning, and collage of spirituality that are influencing and shaping the lifestyles and decisions of ordinary people and community leaders. Only then can you revise or focus the Scriptures to address the spiritual yearning of the public.

The Worship Scriptures and Themes

The Seeker Cycle concentrates on a single story, passage, or extended text in any given worship service. These are the fifty-two passages of the Bible every Christian should know. Presumably, if someone attended every worship service in the year, one would be introduced to all of them. Realistically, that won't happen. The cycle is repeated in the same pattern each year so that people can catch up. Since the Seeker Cycle aims to present the gospel in the learning methodologies of the real public, the church may well employ a strategy of *recap and rerun:*

- *Recap* means that a brief verbal or video synopsis of the previous week precedes the worship service this week. This is particularly helpful if the cultural moment with which the church is in dialogue is an extended event like sports play-offs or festivals.
- *Rerun* means that a complete worship service can be videotaped, burned onto DVD, and edited by the church to be given away or sold to anyone who missed the original event. This is particularly helpful for those who routinely miss worship for certain weeks in the year.

As you scan the scriptures and worship themes in the second and fourth columns of the chart, you will see that twenty-six scriptures are from the Old Testament and twenty-six are from the New Testament. These are intentionally addressed when it seems most appropriate for the spiritual calendar of the public.

One of the most common questions is why *these* passages have been chosen as essential and not others. No doubt there is subjectivity to my choice of scriptures. Choices have been made out of my twenty-five plus years of experience as a pastor; out of dialogue with clergy and laity who have been credible spiritual leaders to congregations; out of feedback from Christian missionaries and church planters when I served as a denominational leader for evangelism and church development; and from my own spiritual journey. These passages have also been tested with my editorial colleagues, including biblical scholars and cultural observers.

Yet my choices are subjective—*and that is precisely the point.* Your local worship design team should feel completely free to add, delete, or change scriptures in the lectionary out of your own experience. This will not be arbitrary or whimsical. It will require spiritual discipline on the part of your team. Just as I have described the spiritual discipline of myself and my team in selecting these scriptures, so also your choices will emerge from deep prayer, extensive Bible study, and deliberate conversation with the many microcultures of your primary mission field. So far, the reaction from the vast majority of churches, from various countries and cultural contexts, is that this list works well.

The Seeker Cycle tries to identify a worship theme for each service. I have only identified the broad topic of the scripture to be used, because no one from outside your primary mission field can really focus the theme of worship in your context at any given time. Your second task as a worship design team will be to revise and focus a single worship theme around which all preaching, singing, praying, drama, or other worship activity will rotate.

You will notice that the stories, passages, or extended texts for each worship service are substantial. Often there are long passages of many verses or even chapters of Scripture. Some stories from the Old and New Testaments are quite lengthy, and the entire story is the focus of worship for that day. The intention is *not* that the entire passage will be read aloud. Perhaps large parts of a story will be dramatized, and only certain verses highlighted for preaching purposes. It is up to the worship design team to spotlight those specific verses, ideas, images, or insights that they perceive to be most relevant to seekers at any given time, in any given year. The same extended text may be treated very differently, with very different focus, over a period of years. The congregation will gather a significant library of print or video perspectives on the same story or passage over time. This allows the worship design team considerable latitude to contextualize the worship service and the text to be most relevant to the people. The Seeker Cycle encourages creativity and flexibility in the design of worship, while still preserving a predictable process with which the church (and all the various musical, dramatic, and personal support teams) can prepare their contributions to worship. For example, worship can be customized to focus on a particular experience of God's grace most needed at a specific time:

• *Healing.* The worship design team may focus the biblical text and worship theme toward the experience of physical, mental, relationship, or spiritual healing for various publics in their primary mission field.
• *Coaching.* The worship design team may focus biblical text and worship themes toward practical guidance as people struggle with ethical ambiguities or lifestyle issues urgent in the everyday experience.
• *Celebration.* The worship design team may focus biblical text and worship themes toward high-energy praise and thanksgiving for grace received, important community breakthroughs, or public events.
• *Cherishing.* The worship design team may focus biblical text and worship themes toward recognition and declaration of eternal truths or core convictions that give hope for tomorrow.

Concentration on a single extended text of Scripture, combined with freedom to spotlight elements of Scripture that most illuminate or guide people in the real time line of their existence, is the strength of the Seeker Cycle.

The desired result of worship in the Seeker Cycle is neither to satisfy intellectual curiosity about Scripture or doctrine, nor is it to make people happy or create emotional good feelings. The desired result is that strangers to grace actually *experience* grace—and that they have a fundamental framework of essential scriptures from the Old and New Testaments with which to make sense of that grace. Just as there is extensive preparation to the design of such worship, so also there is extensive follow-up to the experience. Postworship hospitality should be just as excellent, relevant to the cultural norms of the public, and provocative of meaningful dialogue. The congregation will need to deploy mentors or missionaries among the people, ready to make contact, answer questions, build relationships, and invite people to go deeper into the exploration of Christian faith.

The Uncommon Lectionary is a world in which there are few rules, but definite missional goals. This lectionary expects worship to be relevant to culture, open to the Spirit, and centered on Christ. There are only five basic rules for worship:

1. *Feel absolutely free to customize for your context!* Both the spiritual calendar of the public, and the specific scriptures and their order of appearance, are open to change. Research the major events in your primary mission field and dialogue with people beyond the church. Whatever changes are made should come from the consensus of the worship design team from their spiritual discernment.

2. *Focus scriptures for the missional purpose of any given worship experience.* Each worship service should have specific goals. For example, worship may be focused on healing, coaching, celebration, cherishing eternal truths, and so on. Create an environment for people to experience God's grace in ways most relevant to their needs. Measure success by listening for stories of personal change, deeper spiritual growth, and renewed involvement in outreach and service.

3. *Spotlight specific portions of the single, extended passage of Scripture.* However you dramatize or present the full biblical story, focus worship on specific images, words, ideas, or verses that the Spirit reveals to be most relevant to the public for whom your heart bursts.

4. *Combine drama, music, and image with the spoken word.* Make worship as interactive as possible, using whatever media or learning methodologies are most familiar to the public for whom worship is designed. Do not rely simply on the written or spoken word. Create a larger environment that communicates the meaning of a biblical story or passage.

5. *Connect worship with follow-up conversations and groups.* How you follow up seeker-sensitive worship is just as important as how you welcome seekers into worship. Deploy mentors, members of the church mature in their faith, to seek conversations with strangers during postworship refreshments. Create small groups on the day of worship, or midweek, that will draw seekers into deeper conversation about the basic Bible texts.

Team Meditation and Worship Design

The Seeker Cycle assumes that a worship design team of spiritually disciplined and broadly credible leaders will be trusted to design the overall plan of worship in any given year, and will take responsibility to customize worship each week. This is so important that the Seeker Cycle provides a separate scripture and theme *specifically* for the meditation of the team. You will recall from the previous chapter that a worship design team is *not* simply a task group of professionals or staff. It is a cell group with a distinct missional purpose.

- Task groups design worship out of the various program pieces recommended by commentaries, planning tools, and other resources. The task group members meet each week to do the business, and move on to other work. Usually, there is a brief prayer, some preliminary sharing, and then they get down to work. Since the Common Lectionary encouraged predictable, repetitive, and uniform processes, the task of the group was often simply inserting music, texts, responsive readings, children's stories, and so on, appropriate to the Christian year, into a static template for worship. For special occasions, there might be some additional discussion about sanctuary decorations or the occasional chancel drama. Fundamentally, task groups rely on the expertise of professionals to design worship for a specific standard of excellence. Task groups develop good worship.
- Worship teams customize worship out of the context of their spiritual lives and their dialogue with the local community. Team members meet to pray extensively, follow their own Bible study discipline, share their life struggles and spiritual victories, reflect on demographic trends or key community issues, and then customize a worship experience that will help people experience grace through healing, coaching, celebration, cherishing, and so on. Worship teams are a specific form of cell group or spiritual growth partnership, the fruit of which is a plan for worship this week. They will not limit themselves by any standardized template for worship, and draw from a wider range of communication and learning methodologies to create environments to experience grace.

Fundamentally, worship teams allow the Holy Spirit to elicit the worship design from the context of their shared spiritual life. Worship teams develop great worship.

In addition to the basic cell-group strategy for extensive intercessory prayer, intimate sharing, constant learning, and common affinity or work, a worship design team will emphasize certain things:

1. Specific intercessory prayer for the identifiable microculture in their primary mission field
2. Careful discussion of emerging issues, trends, or challenges in the primary mission field
3. Review of the many different options available to focus the gospel to connect with culture

Clearly, this cell-group gathering takes longer, and requires more personal commitment from the participants, than the average task group. The Seeker Cycle of the Uncommon Lectionary provides a separate Scripture for team meditation and discussion. Sometimes this scripture helps the team reflect on the mission to the targeted needs of their context. Sometimes this Scripture helps them reflect on their role as missionaries and leaders. And sometimes these Scriptures help the worship design team address challenges within their hearts or within their church context that must be overcome in order to persist in mission.

Almost all of the scriptures for team meditation are taken from the Gospel of Luke and the Acts of the Apostles. Again, this may seem like a subjective choice, but it is not an arbitrary one. The Seeker Cycle is intentionally modeled after the earliest church experience of the mission to the Gentiles, and it makes sense that Scriptures from that experience focus the worship design team.

Passages from the Gospel of Luke help keep the team Christ-centered. After all, the goal of the Seeker Cycle is not to transform worshipers into theologians, or members into biblical scholars, or ordinary people into intellectuals. The goal is help them discover a relationship with Jesus Christ, and provide them with a basic biblical foundation to help them interpret what that relationship might mean at any given time, place, or context. Luke's version of the gospel is intentionally designed to interface with the mission to the Gentiles, and to help "God-fearers" understand and respond to the story of

Jesus. It also emphasized the birth of Jesus and the experience of incarnation, which connects well with worship understood as the intersection of the finite and the infinite. No doubt other Gospels are also very important—and in some contexts even more important. Luke's Gospel, however, is more clearly missional than any other Gospel.

Passages from the Acts of the Apostles help the team remain open to the power and unpredictability of the Holy Spirit. Worship teams inevitably experience more adversity and controversy than the professional task groups of the Common Lectionary, because they are obliged to risk more of their spiritual lives in worship and accelerate creativity to reach the public. When they succeed, they succeed gloriously. When they fail, they can fail miserably. The story of the Acts of the Apostles is just such a story, and it gives them encouragement for the journey. More than this, the Acts of the Apostles has much to teach any worship team about principles and tactics for evangelism, outreach, and mission. It is not a story of professionals, but of amateurs who learn as they go.

The Seeker Cycle assumes that the worship team is a handpicked group of credible, spiritual leaders who feel passionate about, and called to, the development of worship that will be relevant to strangers from grace. Most commonly, the pastor handpicks the team. They are chosen because they share commitment to the mission of worship; are prepared to apply or learn, and interface skills to develop great worship; and are ready to hold one another accountable for personal growth and mission results. Team members are not elected or nominated, and they do not represent any particular group or constituency in the church or community. Leaders are not on the team simply by virtue of an office or staff position.

Three key positions on the worship design team will be a message shaper (often the pastor), a music coordinator (often an organist or band leader), and a process developer (often a drama coach or person skilled in making worship as seamless and interactive as possible). These people may or may not be on staff, but it makes sense that if people are on staff as a preacher, musician, or liturgist, they should be *fit to be on the team*. That is to say, they should understand the difference between a worship team and a mere task group, share the mission purpose of the team, and be willing to work together as a team. If they are not fit to be on the team, they should not be on staff in the first place. The team will have to ignore them, or circumvent them anyway. Assuming they are fit to be on the team, they will work together at a more profound level than any mere "professional" relationship.

In addition to these three key positions, the worship design team may well have additional people who contribute to the team in unique ways. These decisions will also be very contextual, varying from place to place and from church to church. Often these additional people will be lay volunteers who are:

- Small-group leaders with high credibility as spiritual guides and mentors
- Outreach leaders with insight into community issues and needs
- Media leaders with expertise in the use of computer generated imaging and projection
- Interior decorators with expertise in shaping floor plans, lighting, and environments
- Specialty music leaders with connections among semi-professional musicians in the community

Not all of these people must be on the core worship design team. Remember that each member of the core team will handpick his or her own team to specifically develop the message, music, and process of worship. All these teams, of course, will function as cell groups or spiritual growth groups. Each group is handpicked by a leader, includes whatever expertise seems necessary for the success of the team's contribution to worship, and is targeted toward the community beyond the church for mission results. Their motto is: *All that matters is the gospel, and everything else is tactics.*

You can see why the issue of reasonable trust is so important for the development and implementation of the Seeker Cycle. Team leaders and their teams need to be very clear about the boundaries of core values, beliefs, vision, and mission beyond which they cannot go. They will be customizing creatively, innovating daringly, and revealing their own spiritual lives vulnerably, and they deserve the trust of the church—just as the church deserves to have reasonable justification to trust them.

The Uncommon Lectionary is a world in which there are few rules, but definite boundaries. This lectionary expects worship teams to model spiritual life and maximize tactical innovation. There are only five basic rules for the worship design team:

1. *Feel absolutely free to think, consult, and create!* The worship team should not feel constrained by the specific calendar, Scriptures,

or themes presented in this chart, or by the specific polity, heritage, or ecclesiastical habits of the church. However, any changes should emerge out of their shared spiritual growth and mission discernment. Nothing should be done without prayerful justification and team consensus.

2. *Interpret the worship theme through team spiritual growth and dialogue with the mission field.* Worship emerges from the spiritual life of the team and their constant conversation with the primary mission field. They stand in between the Holy Spirit and culture. This demands faithfulness, courage, and personal alignment with the vision and mission of the church.

3. *Seek God's guidance to isolate key words and phrases of unusual relevance.* Biblical passages for worship theme or team meditation are large. Spotlight the passages that seem most relevant at any given time and place. Allow the Bible to speak to you, just as you allow the culture to speak to you.

4. *Mobilize additional teams to develop and deliver the message.* Multiply other teams to develop elements of worship as needed. However, be sure to handpick these teams based on commitment, ability to learn and interface skills, and readiness to be held accountable for mission results.

5. *Immediately mingle with people following worship to coach and gain feedback.* Worship team members should be available and approachable at all times before, during, and after worship. They must be able to readily articulate the core values, beliefs, vision, and mission with which they live. They immediately mingle with participants in worship to measure success and gather suggestions to improve worship the next time.

The most important quality identifiable in the hearts of worship team members, which should be instantly recognizable by both members and strangers, is their sense of *urgency*. Worship teams are impatient and eager to help people experience the transformational power of grace, and form a relationship with Jesus Christ.

Old Trinity Church

Old Trinity Church spent considerable time and effort to shift the attitudes of staff, board, and key leaders of the church to understand the urgency for outreach. The most difficult challenge was to help veteran church members understand that worship, too, was all about mission. The Women's Group complained, "But I thought worship was only about praising God!" Pastor John and his associate replied, "What better way for you to praise God than to develop a worship strategy that will get your husband, children, and grandchildren back to worship and deep into faith?" In the end, more than a few members of the church never did understand worship as mission—but once they were assured there would always be an excellent option for traditional worship based on the Common Lectionary they were willing to try.

Pastor John wisely concentrated his persuasion on staff and leaders of the church. The fact that the longtime organist/choir director decided to retire was a particular blessing, and John invested a great deal of attention to the hiring of a new person. As it happened, the assistant organist/choir director proved to be too easily manipulated by past politics, and too comfortable with old habits, and the church made a clean sweep of staffing in the music area. The secretary never fully understood the emerging worship strategy, but she proved very capable in articulating and modeling the core values, beliefs, vision, and mission of the church. And the new part-time church administrator came from an entrepreneurial business background with the United Way, understood perfectly where the church was going, and took over all the negotiations with the trustees and property committees about future renovations and technology upgrades.

The combined coaching of the senior and associate pastor helped the board begin to build clarity and consensus regarding core values, beliefs, vision, and mission. This mollified the worship committee to a considerable extent, and developed a foundation of reasonable trust for the future innovations in worship. Still, there was plenty of skepticism on the part of the worship committee and a pronounced anxiety over loss of control. Their real fear was not that the new worship plan would fail, but that it would be successful.

"If we have too many new people in the church all at once," they worried, "crazy, theologically unsound, potentially expensive, or even immoral things might happen!" John led an extensive Bible study on the two letters of Paul to the Corinthians (where crazy, theologically unsound, and immoral things did break out) and talked about how Paul addressed these problems by clarifying the fruits of the Spirit and bedrock convictions of faith. The committee

adopted a wait-and-see attitude. John took what he could get but knew there would still be conflict down the road.

The stage was now set to form the first worship design team. The Seeker Cycle was shared with staff and volunteer leaders, but John wisely resisted the temptation to start critiquing and revising the lectionary right away, and he resisted the temptation to gather a few staff and create a seeker-sensitive worship service from scratch.

"It must emerge from the spiritual growth of the team," his wife wisely counseled. "First get the right team, and the program will follow from that."

This was not easy for John. After all, he felt that he was a professional, that he knew what he was doing, that he was already a pretty sensitive guy, and besides, if anyone should take criticism it should be him. He was the chief, and it was hard for John to acknowledge he might need to grow, change, and learn like everyone else.

John picked his team with care. He would fulfill the role of message shaper. His new music director would fulfill the role of music coordinator. His associate minister did have skills in worship process, and had remarkable sensitivity to the Hispanic community growing around them, so she joined the team as process developer. Since none of them had ever previously worked as part of a real, true team (they had only participated in task groups that were called teams), they jointly took some training through a community college course for nonprofit organizations (no seminaries currently having anything remotely like team development in their continuing education curriculums).

John then added three lay volunteers to the design team who were passionate about worship. Two were small-group leaders involved with adult faith formation, and the third was a seventeen-year-old with more knowledge of media than anybody else in the church.

The team began to meet as a cell group, following a typical process of prayer, Bible study (using the Scriptures for team meditation and worship theme), conversation with culture, intimate sharing, and so on. It took about nine weeks for the first major conflict to erupt.

Commentary

Conflict came as a surprise to John. He had expected it with leaders or members who did not understand worship as mission, but he had not expected it among the members of the team who shared the passion. His mistake came from confusion between passion and calling. The team members were passionate about worship, but not all of them felt clearly called into mission. One team member in particular was excited about creating contemporary worship, but it was still oriented around his personal tastes, family needs, and political perspectives and those of his friends. He could not sacrifice *his* personal preferences for the sake of microcultures who were outside his demographic and lifestyle circle of relationships.

John realized that he had also failed to establish a time line for evaluation and closure for team membership. This made it doubly difficult to remove a team member who did not interface with the real mission of the team. However, remembering his previous mistake with the senior organist/choir director, he moved quickly to confront the problem and replace this member of the team.

Now that the mission focus of worship was clearly owned by the entire team, they worked quickly to fill in the spiritual calendar of the public in their primary mission field. They studied demographics and trends and compared lifestyle segments. They also interviewed senior planners in the retail, food, entertainment, and sports industries. Initially, they did so only to clarify the dates of major events, or the timing for marketing. To their surprise, they found these leaders remarkably eager to talk with them. These people, too, were among the seekers or God-fearers who felt out of place in worship based on the Common Lectionary, but who were quite interested to learn how the gospel could connect with culture as they experienced it. John and his team made notes for future reference indicating specific ways these leaders might contribute to the actual development, implementation, and marketing of the Seeker Cycle of worship.

Having completed the calendar, they now began to refine or adjust the Scriptures and worship themes for each week. The laity on the team were new to this, because they never imagined that worship could be, or should be, planned months in advance. John, of course, was used to this. His habit with the Common Lectionary was to do similar planning in August for the coming program year. Everyone realized that in order to empower various teams for music, technology, drama, refreshments, and more, the worship design team needed to provide them with advanced notice and basic guidance about the message, environment, and experience of grace they wanted any given worship service to convey.

Commentary

John and his associate minister soon discovered that they, personally, faced a huge learning curve. Although they understood theoretically what a seeker-sensitive worship service was about, their whole background in the church and seminary training had done little to equip them to do it. They were trapped by words—or by wordiness. They could only think in terms of oral or written communication, and this wordy, linear, abstract method of communication could only happen through structured prayers, responsive readings, and hard copy books and handouts.

"OK, let's work on the order of service," they said. And they were shocked when the music coordinator and technology teenager looked at them and said, "What order of service? Why would we want to give out any paper at all? Who said you were going to preach?"

John's team educated him to understand that the general public actually relies on several distinct learning methodologies. In order of importance, they are:

1. Images, movie clips, television spots, sound bites, and songs
2. Conversations, relationships, drama, modeling, and behavior modification
3. Brief reading from newspapers, magazines, Web sites, and e-mail
4. Books, lectures, sermons, and hard copy

Earlier I called attention to the greeting card business. Today, the number of spiritual moments celebrated among the public are so diverse and are changing so fast, that many greeting cards are blank. They contain no words at all, but only an image. It may be black and white, or holographic, but they are rarely just diagrams or clip art. Indeed, the "real" greeting cards are being replaced by virtual greeting cards that are delivered over the Internet as e-mail and invite interaction. The principles are directly transferable to the design of missional worship in the Seeker Cycle.

Although John's heart was in the right place, his *habits* were still with the Common Lectionary. He was still a communication technician, and God was calling him to be a communication artist. Fortunately, his music and technology team members, and his team members with small-group leadership backgrounds, came to his rescue.

The more John and his team redefined their work as art rather than science, the more excited and terrified they became. They were excited, because they sensed that worship as art would allow far more interventions of the

Holy and powerful experiences of grace than worship as words ever did. They began to rethink the drama of worship, and return to Christian history to recapture the drama of the sacraments. Yet they also were terrified because they realized that the tactics to develop great worship had just multiplied exponentially—and they felt very inadequate.

"Wouldn't it be great," said the youngest team member, "if during the community carnival in August we could celebrate a baptism dramatized as the leap of faith? We could contract with a high dive act and hold the baptism in our parking lot. Get one of those real tall ladders and diving boards with the small pool of water far below. Imagine the diver, dressed all in white. We pray; we sing; we praise God. As the drum rolls, the diver slowly climbs to the top. A big sign on the ladder says, 'This is you!' A big sign on the pool of water says, 'This is grace!' We lead the whole crowd to say the Lord's Prayer. The diver plummets fifty feet; the splash gets everybody wet. And over the loudspeakers, at the highest volume, we've got our organist and choir ready to plunge into the Hallelujah Chorus!"

"Oh! Oh!" says one of the older team members. "And we could pour kerosene onto the pool of water and light it with fire, just before the jump. Maybe we could do it at night! It could dramatize even more the extinguishing of sin and the hope of salvation. And we could ask our church elders to all wear bathing suits, marking them as baptized Christians who have already made the leap, so that people could go up and talk to them."

"I'm not sure the trustees would go for it," commented another team member skeptically.

"The liability insurance issues can be sorted out," said the associate pastor. "I'm sure that retail mall developer who holds the carnival in his mall parking lot could help us figure that out. And what could the trustees really say? It's wild, but it's still within the boundaries of our church core values, beliefs, vision, and mission."

"Well," said John, "we could also buy a large quantity of plush toys with the theme of diving and water, and have the Scripture text for that day engraved on the front, and the name of our church and our mission statement engraved on the back. And we could give them away!" John was beginning to get into this alternative learning methodology stuff.

Team conversations kept getting more and more creative, as the team pondered how to help seekers really see, touch, smell, hear, taste, and fully experience the grace of God. It was vitally important to them, however, that the goal of acquainting seekers with the fifty-two Bible passages every Christian should know succeeded. This did involve words and abstract ideas. The team developed a policy to govern all of its work: "We will never share a biblical text without providing some additional experience to reinforce the message of the text, and we will never offer a spiritual experience without providing in oral or written form the words of Scripture."

With that principle in mind, they began to focus the message, and customize the process, and design the images and music and drama, for each week in the lectionary.

Commentary

The Uncommon Lectionary requires a database for resources just as much as the Common Lectionary. The content of that database has shifted both in the nature of the material and in the proportions of material.

The database for the Common Lectionary relied heavily on commentaries by scholars, sermons from well-known preachers, historical anecdotes of famous people or Christian leaders, quotations from great literature, and so on. Lectionary helps for each of the three years of the cycles provided personal reflections from various people, stories from global or national missions, insight into relevant world events, and occasional insights into various cultures or disciplines. Preachers accumulated libraries, print or digital, that are searchable by keyword and topic. Denominations provided information to connect the Christian year with their own heritage and practices. Local ministerials formed lectionary discussion groups.

The database for the Uncommon Lectionary includes biblical commentaries and historical insights, but is overbalanced in three other directions: media, networks, and spiritual disciplines. This database will be developed by each worship design team and grow significantly over time. The database can be shared among churches and church leaders, but it is not as transferable as the database for the Common Lectionary. The pastor could literally move his or her library to a new church and use the database intact. Now, the database is too connected with the context and cultures of the primary mission field to be automatically transferable. The media, networks, and spiritual disciplines require constant upgrading to maintain relevance.

The media database developed by the worship design team will be a combination of borrowed and contextually developed material. Borrowed material will often require copyright permission to use, and part of the database will be lists of addresses or owners whose permission must be gained to use the media. If there is a cost, that is part of the worship budget, just as choral music is part of the budget for the Common Lectionary.

- Still images, black and white or color, will be needed for computer generated projections and all kinds of interior decorations, brochures, marketing, and so on. These images are generally of two kinds: background images against which words and music can be placed to enhance the meaning of the words; and images that capture the movement of culture or the essence of Scripture. These are the pictures that are worth a thousand words. Note that these images are *not* often images from nature (sunsets, flowers, mountain vistas, and so on). The images you want are of people, faces, activities, events, culture, and action. Many of these images should be taken locally, by amateur digital photographers from your own community, and depict the primary mission field of the church.

- Video and movie clips will be needed for sermon illustrations, meditation focus, and prayer. Some of these movie clips may be stored; others may simply be references to resources the worship design team will have to individually download or obtain. Both contemporary and old movies can be excellent resources. The choices will be guided by your sensitivity to the microcultures in your primary mission field. As digital photography dramatically improves, churches need to develop their own amateur video clips. These may be ten seconds to five minutes in length. The amateur quality actually enhances the authenticity and relevance of the video.

- Music, in every genre, is a crucial part of the database. This does include classical music, jazz, blues, R & B, opera, rap, and any music that is heard over the radio in your primary mission field. It may not be possible to keep copies of entire songs in the database, but an index of titles, key lyrics, or topics will be crucial. Copyright permission to use music varies considerably among distributors, and the database should include not only the contact to obtain permission, but a record of the cost and time line required to get the permission.

- Recorded dialogue, man on the street interviews, and other audio or video clips will be included in the database. For example, if the senior pastor interviews a municipal planner, nonprofit CEO, church leader, or other community person, the church can edit several clips that can be used for multiple purposes or in multiple worship services. These can be broadcast or projected easily in basic software programs.

• In addition to media for sound and sight, the database should include ideas or resources related to taste, touch, and smell. This will help worship designers create environments for meditation, conversation, learning, and so on.

The media database will include resources for chancel drama, dance, unusual musical ensembles and instrumentations, and any strategy that will help make worship more interactive or culturally relevant.

The network database should be intentionally cross-disciplinary and cross-denominational. It will include Web sites from publishers, churches, parachurches, nonprofit organizations, and other groups that are particularly relevant to the mission. These are not just networks compatible with the values, beliefs, vision, and mission of the church. These are Web sites *frequently visited by the public in your primary mission field.* Regardless how offensive or incompatible these networks might be, it is important for worship designers to know who is influencing the thought and behavior of the public and how. There are also e-mail forums that provide coaching and advice for churches in worship design or mission outreach.

In addition to Web site networks, there are other face-to-face networks or local contacts that are useful to maintain. In John's team meeting described above, it would be helpful if the team could immediately find in their database a local source for plush toys and carnival-style gifts that can be purchased wholesale. Networks that link the church to retail, entertainment, and sports event planners will be crucial. The church needs to be in ongoing conversation with other churches following similar paths of mission.

The database for spiritual discipline is perhaps the most surprising, and yet the most crucial database of all. In the Uncommon Lectionary, worship emerges from the continuing spiritual growth of the worship design team—not from top-down directives about what scriptures should be preached on specific topics related to the Christian year. The Common Lectionary demands professional knowledge and institutional allegiance. The Uncommon Lectionary demands constant spiritual growth and cross-cultural conversation.

The database for spiritual discipline will include two kinds of resources. The first are resources from the whole history of the church. These are disciplines from both before and after the printing press. They may involve reading and reflection, but also devotional objects, meditation practices, and spiritual partnerships. The second are resources that empower and enhance any form of cross-cultural dialogue. These may involve study of other disciplines or cultures, or actual conversation with leaders in other disciplines or members of other cultures.

The catalogue for spiritual discipline should include any tactic that might in foreseeable ways help the worship design team go deeper, leap farther, climb higher, or be stiller. For example, strategies can include ancient reflection on the seven deadly sins and seven lively virtues, guided Ignatian prayer, the Rule of Saint Benedict, the spiritual questions of John Wesley, the practice of twelve-step programs, mystical contemplation, and on and on. Or for example, strategies might include disciplines for listening, behavioral norms for different cultures, corporate expectations for entrepreneurial businesses, and on and on. The point is that what makes Seeker Cycle worship *relevant* is not simply updated media files or ongoing networked conversations, but the ability of the team to constantly challenge their own comfort zones and allow the Holy Spirit to take them farther.

Old Trinity Church launched their Seeker Cycle worship service with the New Year in January. From August through December, the team had shaped and planned the worship services that would address the spiritual calendar of the public. They consolidated the traditional service based on the Common Lectionary into the 11:00 service on Sunday morning, believing that this constituency would be driving downtown to church from some miles away and would require additional time to get to church. They launched the Seeker Cycle service at 9:30, believing that this constituency would be closer and want to finish church in good time to enjoy the rest of the day. They also wanted to keep the Seeker service prime time on Sunday morning, because in their primary mission field that was when seekers were most likely going to explore religion. This time, John made a point of naming a time line and providing a mechanism to make adjustments in the schedule if required.

One of the unexpected dilemmas was what to do for Easter and Christmas Eve. These classic services brought so many people expecting a traditional, Common Lectionary–based service that they could not be contained in just a single Sunday morning service at Easter or a single evening service at

Christmas. There was mounting pressure to cancel or blend in the Seeker Cycle service.

John recognized that this was not just a practical problem, but a symbolic challenge to the Seeker Cycle that could have lasting implications. If Old Trinity cancelled or blended in the Seeker Cycle, it would openly declare that one constituency was more important than another and that worship was still, in the end, all about membership assimilation rather missional outreach. Already there were voices whispering in the hallways that at least, at Easter and Christmas, the "baby" worship service would end and people would have to "mature" by participating in the "regular" worship service.

By now, John, the staff, and the core leaders of the board were united in their support of the Seeker Cycle as an equally valid alternative to the Common Lectionary. Their solution was to add a third service in the afternoon on Easter that would duplicate the 11:00 service, with an elaborate lunch in between. For Christmas, they chose to launch a special Seeker's Christmas service a week before Christmas Eve, convinced that many of the people they wanted to reach would not want to interrupt their personal and family festivities on Christmas Eve anyway.

The whole exercise also prompted the worship design team to think even further out of the box. In order to supplement the plan for the Seeker Cycle service on Sundays, they decided to plan major community Seeker celebrations on three other occasions in the spiritual calendar of the public (in addition to the week before Christmas). These celebrations would be on Valentine's Day, the citywide cross-cultural carnival in August, and Halloween.

The worship design team began to settle into a rhythm. They knew that they could only go into so much detail too far in advance, so they established a four-month production schedule. In doing so, they could give four months notice to all of their various teams to develop components for coming worship services. The team routine was to meet every Monday morning promptly at 9:00. This disrupted John's habit for Monday off, but his habits were less important than providing volunteers with ample lead time to prepare for worship. The meeting began with extensive intercessory prayer for people who were strangers to grace in their primary mission field, and then continued as follows:

- *Updates from individual team members regarding their spiritual journey or growth, life struggles, and spiritual victories*
- *Discussion of the Uncommon Lectionary text for team meditation*
- *Report and discussion of recent demographic research or conversations with community leaders or residents about needs, issues, concerns, and so on*

- *Discussion of the worship theme for the coming Sunday service*
- *Refinement of the message, music, and worship process for Sunday, with attention to any special interactive features to the service, or any special instructions for the various musical groups, technology teams, or personal support teams*
- *Review of the coming worship services four months ahead to add detail, raise key questions, and coordinate activities*

The team concluded their meeting with lunch together. They lunched outside of the church building, in a different restaurant, food court, or deli every time, so that they could continue to immerse themselves in the many cultures of the community, and continue to share their spiritual growth and mission insights with one another.

Old Trinity Church began to change. The Seeker Cycle plan and worship design team routine changed and adapted over time, but after two years church leaders and members had become accustomed to a new, mission-driven way of thinking. The staff never felt more alive and effective. The interaction with the cultures of the primary mission field spilled over into the traditional Common Lectionary service to give it new energy and focus as well.

As the Seeker Cycle service grew, it drove the worship design team to plan more intentionally their hospitality ministries and follow-up tactics. They began to attract newcomers who were ever more wary of religious institutions, and had to be even more sensitive to welcome them without judgment or preconception. They also began to succeed in helping people experience grace, and needed to be even more creative to find ways to draw these "strangers" into a closer community of learning and growth. One of the greatest, albeit hidden, benefits of the Seeker Cycle was that many of the longtime church members began to participate in both the Seeker service and the Common Lectionary service and for the first time became truly familiar with the fifty-two Bible passages every Christian should know.

Yet after two years, John, his staff, and the leaders of Old Trinity Church came to a startling conclusion. The Seeker Cycle service was growing in spiritual depth, mission impact, and numbers. The traditional Common Lectionary service was also growing in spiritual depth—but not in cultural diversity or numbers! In other words, although the Common Lectionary service was still vital and effective for some people, it was not really seen as the next step in spiritual growth and worship for many of the seekers who had come to know Christ and build a biblical foundation for living. Old Trinity Church needed yet another alternative.

CHAPTER FIVE

The Disciple Cycle

The Disciple Cycle is designed to build on the foundation of the Seeker Cycle. It assumes that worship participants who have once been strangers to grace are strangers no longer, and that they have a foundational knowledge of the basic passages of the Bible with which to interpret those experiences of grace. So far their lives are not particularly disciplined to go deeper into faith, hope, and Christian lifestyle—but the desire or motivation to go deeper has begun to emerge.

The Disciple Cycle is modeled after the mentoring process of the apostles and the later monastic experience of the fourth through tenth centuries.

- The apostles personally passed on their transformational experience with Jesus, memory of Christ's Great Commission and commandments, understanding of the teaching of the Old Testament and gospel, and insight into the working of the Holy Spirit in contemporary times. They gathered disciples around them who would preserve the teaching and imitate their teacher so well that they could even use the teacher's name in addressing epistles to their own followers. The existence of several letters by "John" or "Peter" is a witness to the effectiveness of such discipling.
- In the fourth through tenth centuries, restless Christians wanting to go deeper into faith, hope, and Christian lifestyle left traditional institutional parishes to form independent communities. This was the beginning of the monastic movement. They gath-

ered around spiritual leaders apart from the distractions of the world to shape a lifestyle around relationships, labor, prayer and meditation, teaching and learning, and service explicitly *centered on the experience of Christ*. Disciples discerned a clearer sense of personal mission, many going forth to be *in* the world (but no longer *of* the world) to become prophets, reformers, educators, healers, and public leaders.

The Disciple Cycle is intended to provide a plan for worship that takes people deeper into a comprehensive knowledge of the salvation history revealed in Scripture. It is centered specifically on the experience of Christ. It is an integral part of a larger mentoring strategy to help people go deeper to explore faith, find hope, and shape their lifestyles around Christ.

Just as Christendom lost clarity about what a seeker really is, so also Christendom lost clarity about what a disciple really is. The Common Lectionary tended to reinforce the notion that a seeker was simply someone outside the institutional church, and that a disciple was a professional clergyperson or a biblically literate church member. The Disciple Cycle assumes a definition of disciple similar to that of the church of the first millennium.

A disciple is one who specifically and articulately follows Jesus Christ. A disciple is one who shapes his or her lifestyle in imitation of Christ; who prioritizes his or her time and energy to receive faith in Christ and understand the faith of Christ; and who locates his or her one hope for abundant life in the experience of Christ and the return of Christ. Moreover, a disciple is one who participates in a process of "discipling." Disciples are dedicated to learning from a credible spiritual guide—so that they might become credible spiritual guides for other people. Every mentor was once a disciple, and every disciple is called to be a mentor. Whether or not a disciple is also a member of an institutional church is a Christendom distinction foreign to the earliest church. Being a member of the mystical body of Christ implies being a disciple, and being a disciple assumes that you accept the mission and obligations of membership in the body of Christ. A disciple is not only one who imitates Christ, but also is one who pursues the mission of Christ, as his or her mentors did before.

It is crucial to understand that the goals of the Disciple Cycle are different from the goals of the Common Lectionary. There the goal was to develop good church members through the experience of good worship. Here the goal is to develop faithful disciples through the experience of great worship.

- The goal is not to make people biblically literate, but to make them biblically conversant. The Disciple Cycle is not trying to teach people the techniques of biblical critical method, acquaint them with the sociology of the ancient Middle East, or compare time lines and theological perspectives. It is intended to help people become so familiar with the biblical stories, metaphors, and ideas that these alter their daily conversations, shape their daily behavior, revise their perceptions of reality, and define their hope for tomorrow. The goal is not to make the Bible understandable in the church parlor or lecture hall, but to make the Bible live in daily life.

- The goal is not to help church members understand diverse theological threads and historical processes with Scripture, but to help disciples build a solid faith that will give them strength in times of confusion or stress. The Disciple Cycle is intended to equip Christians to lead a lifestyle that is different from the rest of the pagan world and to endure the struggles and challenges that will inevitably come because of it. Ultimately, the goal is not to impart knowledge, but to provide reasonable hope for the future. The debate between faith and knowledge is a Christendom debate. The debate that rages in a post-Christendom world is between mere knowledge and real hope. The Disciple Cycle is designed to provide real hope.

- The goal is not to place Jesus in historical context, nor even to apply Jesus' teachings to contemporary dilemmas. The goal is to experience Jesus. The Disciple Cycle is designed to bring people into the presence of Christ, and to involve them in a process of salvation history that began with the first man and woman alienated from grace, and will only end when the last man and woman are reunited with grace. The experience of Christ, the flow of the spirit, and the immediacy of God are all implied by the word *relationship*. Relationship with Christ means participating in many facets of divine grace, and sharing the ongoing mission of Christ.

The Disciple Cycle is the natural next step to the Seeker Cycle. The traditional worship of the Common Lectionary cannot do this. Strangers to grace who have come to experience God and build a biblical foundation to interpret the experience do not readily "graduate" to the Common Lectionary. The goals are simply different from their goals. This is not to say that the Common Lectionary will not be relevant in other ways and at other times in their spiritual journeys. It is simply to say that their priority is not to become students of the Bible and learned theologians, but mentors of grace and disciples of Jesus.

The Disciple Cycle is more complicated than the Seeker Cycle. Like the Seeker Cycle, it is a fifty-two-week plan for preaching and worship that focuses on a single extended biblical text each week and is repeated annually. It requires a worship design team, and provides the team with a relevant biblical text for their own meditation. However, in addition to this, the Disciple Cycle assumes (indeed, *expects*) that the vast majority of worshipers will participate in intentional small-group discussions that follow up on the theme of worship. An additional Scripture is provided for the focused discussion of these small groups. Moreover, the worship and small-group discussion are specifically guided to reflect on the experience of Jesus Christ and the spiritual life.

The Disciple Cycle is not for the dilettante. In the Seeker Cycle, anyone is welcome, with no strings attached. No one will ever ask you to reconsider your commitment to attend or encourage you to drop out. In the Disciple Cycle, this is reversed. There is a clear, motivational prerequisite. People are encouraged to attend the Disciple Cycle worship service *only* if they are prepared to participate in the small groups that follow. If not, they are specifically encouraged *not* to attend the worship service.

This seems counterintuitive to most church people raised in the era of Christendom—and especially in the latter days of Christendom when any warm body is welcome to sit in the pew. However, postmodern people (like ancient people) actually welcome and appreciate a higher standard of expectation. If they go to university, they are expected to rise to a certain standard of commitment. If they work for any great business, they are expected to rise to a certain standard of performance. If they were *not* asked to raise their personal standards, they would assume the university or company must not be very good in the first place. The same reasoning is brought to the church. People prefer higher standards when it comes to religion. The prerequisite, in the case of the church, is desire or motivation. If people do not *desire* to go deep into faith, hope, and lifestyle, if they do not *desire* to know Christ more deeply and powerfully, then they will not want to obligate themselves to additional postworship small groups. If they do desire this, they will. The choice is similar to the one posed so long ago in the monastic movement of the fourth through tenth centuries. The rigor of the monastic community may not be for everyone—but it is exactly right for those who desire it most. And these are the future leaders, mentors, and disciples who will grow the church, expand the mission, and change the world.

It might be useful to leap ahead and provide a snapshot of the two cycles of worship in action, in order to help the reader understand the different goals and strategies of the Disciple Cycle.

Old Trinity Church

Pastor John and the Old Trinity Church team cast a vision of what worship might look like five years into the future.

They assumed that they would still have a Common Lectionary worship service at 11:00 on Sunday morning. Anyone and everyone would be welcome to attend. The worship service would be traditional in that it would follow the Christian year, include good liturgy and expository preaching, and provide inspirational performances in fairly classical genres of music. Everyone expected the Common Lectionary service to communicate denominational policy and distinctiveness; provide knowledge about the sources, perspectives, and ideas of Scripture; and assimilate people into the institutional church and its programs.

They imagined that the Seeker Cycle service would continue to be at 9:30 on Sunday morning, and look something like this: People would come as they were to the renovated gymnasium for worship. (Note: The team realized that the formal sanctuary would be inadequate for the Seeker Cycle service, because there was no way to create environments with image, sound, and interaction without expensive renovation and major conflict. It was easier to dramatically renovate the gym into a worship center—and relocate youth basketball to the YMCA. The church negotiated a weekly reservation, and paid for the exclusive use of the YMCA facilities by the church. Interestingly, as soon as the youth ministry was located away from the church building, it doubled in size.)

Great hospitality greeted people as they entered worship. Refreshments were served constantly, the music was already going, and people sat around tables or in comfortable chairs. The service was very visual or sensory with lots of inter-

action. The single biblical passage or text was shared in multiple media, interpreted in the context of the spiritual calendar of the public, and oriented to healing, coaching, cherishing, or celebration. People were usually deeply moved and appreciated learning about a vital "chunk" of Scripture. Many connected with mentors after the service to talk, and some attended other learning experiences during the week. Everybody and anybody was welcome; the church assumed no background knowledge whatsoever, and earnestly wanted to introduce these strangers to grace to an experience that would give them new life.

They imagined that the Disciple Cycle service would continue at 12:30. A simple lunch could be purchased for about 10 percent more than the deli down the street, with the money going to a local mission outreach. Worship was held in the renovated gymnasium. This was because they expected every participant would bring a Bible and a notebook, and require either a table or sufficient personal space to do work. Many would bring laptop computers, so the gymnasium renovation included installation of numerous electrical outlets in the floor to reduce the number of cords that might trip people. The service was still come as you are, with plenty of refreshments, but there was a new seriousness of purpose. If people did not bring a Bible, they were provided with one at the door. If they did not already have midweek small group, an usher sat down with them to assign the group that was at a time, place, or relationship most convenient to the worshiper.

The worship began with extensive prayer, in one of many different forms, with background music, sound effects, images, incense, and body movement (holding hands, upraised arms, and people on their knees, and so on). Songs might be in any musical genre, but the lyrics were very important and always projected. Worship on any given Sunday was actually part of a larger story line of Scripture lasting two to three months, necessitating recaps and previews. The message was based on a single, extensive passage and would be shared in a variety of media— but the mentoring lasted an average of forty-five minutes as people took notes and broke into brief table group discussions. Anyone could interrupt at any time with a question, and wireless Internet access linked the really timid to an exclusive Web site with downloadable images and a simple message board. Typed questions would immediately appear on the open computer in front of the message giver, so that he could immediately pause and answer the question. Since Eucharist was part of the bedrock beliefs of Old Trinity Church, it was celebrated in any number of ways in every worship service of the Disciple Cycle.

Worship in the Disciple Cycle always linked to reflection on the experience of Christ, and always contained coaching for the spiritual life. Worship participants often sat with their small groups (not their families). Before the close of worship, everyone was expected to gather in his or her small group to hold hands for the benediction, and recovenant to participate in the small group that week. Any special study material and any other news or announcements about the church were shared at that time. The Old Trinity Church team anticipated that worship might end about 2:00, having lasted about one and a half hours.

The Old Trinity Church team imagined that the largest attendance for worship would be with the Seeker Cycle service. At any given time, the proportion would be about 60 percent newcomers or adherents and about 40 percent church members. The Common Lectionary service would maintain its current numbers. At any given time, the proportion would be about 10 percent newcomers and 90 percent members. The Disciple Cycle service would be the smallest and most intimate worship experience. All staff, board members, trustees, and Sunday school teachers were required to attend. The proportion would be about 100 percent members, with a sprinkling of leaders and members from other churches who wanted to go deep.

The Worship Design Team

The work and routine of the worship design team explained in the Seeker Cycle are repeated in the Disciple Cycle. However, since the Disciple Cycle has a different goal and is more complicated to design, it is not possible for the same team to design both worship services. If a church is running simultaneous Seeker Cycle and Disciple Cycle services, it must develop two distinct design teams. Even if a smaller church deploys the two cycles in alternate or rotating years, the team that works well with one cycle may not be the team that will work well with the other. The cycles have very different goals, and will be supported by a different sense of passion and call, that requires different skills.

Clearly, the design team and the actual leadership teams that implement each worship service will become ever more distinct over time. The contextual relevance of any given Seeker Cycle service, or the story line of any given Disciple Cycle service, may well demand different leaders to share the message, perform the music, or develop the process of worship. As the model of worship develops, even the senior pastor may not be able to have all the abilities, or find sufficient time, to design and lead all the worship options. Either paid or unpaid leaders will need to share more and more of the workload for worship.

This "de-professionalizing" of worship design and leadership may again be counterintuitive for clergy and church members raised in

Christendom. They will have worries about the quality and integrity of worship. Therefore, the church will need to provide larger continuing education budgets to train people in worship design and leadership, and be very clear about their consensus regarding values, beliefs, vision, and mission. Yet this should not be surprising. The "deprofessionalizing" of worship was exactly what happened in the early church of the first millennium, and was the original intent of the Reformation conviction of the priesthood of all believers.

The additional work of the design and leadership teams will become clearer as we describe the details of the Disciple Cycle. Please refer to the appendix B chart that outlines the schedule and plan of worship.

The Organization of the Calendar Year

The Disciple Cycle organizes the calendar year in two ways. It does not refer to the Christian year. It is designed to connect the great themes of Scripture with the flow of everyday life.

First, it follows the flow of experience that is typical for the public today as they anticipate regular changes in their lifestyles. The Seeker Cycle concentrates on the "high spiritual moments" or "holy days" that punctuate the spiritual calendar of the public. However, the Disciple Cycle concentrates on the typical movement of life in between and through these particular moments. The flow of life is dictated by public school calendars, retail and business strategic planning, seasons of the year, summer holidays, family life cycles, group sports and activities, and so on. The Disciple Cycle does not ask people to make exceptions to that routine in order to connect with worship, but enables them to integrate their spiritual life and learning with the routine of their annual calendar.

Second, the Disciple Cycle divides the year into five major story lines that comprehensively cover the entire Bible and capture the significance of salvation history from the perspective of Christian faith. These themes are identified on the appendix B chart in the column to the far right. Compare these to the actual weeks of the year (numbered from the first week in January) in the column on the far left. For the sake of worship planning, it logically makes sense to begin with "Israel's Covenant" and work forward from this point.

At first, it may seem confusing to start worship planning with week 19 in the month of May. However, if you reflect on how the five story lines of Scripture interface with real life, it makes perfect sense. The end of May actually marks a decisive change in lifestyle for the public in the Northern Hemisphere. Spring is in full bloom; public schools, universities, and continuing education schedules change; work schedules are radically altered. It makes sense to explore the story line that begins with creation and anticipates the promised land. Similarly, it makes sense to conclude the planning cycle with the resurrection, ascension, and Great Commission of Christ as the basis of the Christian mission that has been the focus of winter and spring.

The planning concept is to start with the origins of creation and covenant, and follow the flow of salvation history all the way through the experience of Christ, Great Commission, and the mission to share the good news. This raises an important question. When, exactly, does the worship design team plan the yearly cycle? The most common practice for the Common Lectionary was to do the worship planning in August. This helped the team focus for the programs restarted in September, and provided about three months' notice for leaders in music, education, and fellowship to prepare for the start of the Christian year in Advent. Even with the Seeker Cycle, the worship team could still plan the year in August, and provide about four months' notice for leaders to prepare for the start of the public calendar in January.

The Disciple Cycle requires a different pattern of planning. The higher expectation for planning on the part of the worship design team parallels the higher expectation for participation of worshipers. Planning for the year should begin in January (not August), thus giving leaders for small groups, Sunday school, fellowship, and outreach three to four months to make their own preparations for the coming cycle. Note that the Common Lectionary and the Seeker Cycle both assume there will be a program hiatus and relaxation of spiritual discipline in the summer. The Disciple Cycle holds the leadership of the church to a higher standard, expecting that worship attendance and spiritual discipline will remain strong throughout the summer. Even if leaders travel from home, they will be expected to keep up with the worship cycle and their small group. The fact that the worship design team does its basic planning in January encourages the team to strategize *through* the summer and not *in spite* of the summer.

I am aware that my description of planning assumes a calendar most familiar to churches in the Northern Hemisphere. Churches in the Southern Hemisphere may well reverse the experience of summer holidays. This only reinforces the need to customize or contextualize the planning for the Disciple Cycle. In the Northern Hemisphere, church attendance typically falls off from mid-May through mid-September. That means the first two story lines of the Disciple Cycle are most likely to be given minimal attention, and the worship team will need to coordinate with small-group leaders to compensate. In the Southern Hemisphere, church attendance typically falls off from January through April, and the last story line of the cycle is most likely to be given minimal attention. This, in fact, is more serious. This last story line is the one that focuses Christian outreach (both personal and corporate mission), which is perhaps an even bigger challenge for Australia, New Zealand, and other countries most influenced by European ways.

How will the church compensate? Fortunately, small groups can customize changes in schedule, and link members via e-mail, with relative ease. Compensating for lost worship attendance due to family and personal travel, however, will lead the church to become more intentional about long-distance learning. The rapid development of interactive Web sites will be crucial to the advanced deployment of the Disciple Cycle. Worship can be edited and added to church Web sites for viewing; message boards can be added that allow dialogue between pastor and participant, or among participants, wherever they are around the world.

The Five Story Lines of Scripture

The Disciple Cycle divides the year into five overarching story lines. The year is actually divided equally between the Old Testament and the New Testament. Preaching and worship concentrate on a distinct story line for three eight- or nine-week periods (through the Old Testament), and two twelve-week periods (through the New Testament). This allows extensive teaching and dialogue for exploring a broad theme of salvation history. The single passages selected for each week are large blocks of Scripture, and the particular focus of the worship design team will no doubt vary from year to year. This gives significant latitude to listen to both spirit and culture, applying the text in both timely and timeless ways.

The five story lines of Scripture try to capture the movement of salvation history from the perspective of Christian faith. The term *salvation history* has gone out of fashion in recent years. Liberals tend to be unclear about *salvation*, and conservatives tend to be unclear about *history*. The premise of the Disciple Cycle of worship is simply that the world became estranged from God and yearns to return; and God overflows with compassion for creation and yearns to redeem it. This is the same principle of the intersection of the finite and the infinite that is the very basis of great worship. There is no particular dogmatic or doctrinal agenda that is assumed by the Disciple Cycle, and it could be interpreted by various Christian perspectives in different ways. The fundamental principle is simply that the fundamental alienation of the world from God is acceptable to neither. Humans yearn for reunion, but cannot ultimately accomplish it; God accomplishes it, but cannot force humanity to accept it.

The origin of this alienation, the conditions of existence, the human and divine methods to overcome it, and the description of the destiny that is promised are all topics for interpretation and discussion in the Disciple Cycle. The first underlying assumption is that salvation is, after all, what Christian faith is all about. That is the point of the whole exercise of religion. Salvation may be defined or experienced in many ways, but unless people have real hope in the victory of God, there is no real point to worship (or the church) in the first place. Better to be a stoic, an epicure, or a lottery winner. The second underlying assumption is that history is, after all, the context in which that salvation is going to happen. That is the struggle of life. History may be interpreted or experienced in many ways, but one way or another the human search for purpose, pattern, logic, and meaning is worthwhile. Salvation is a process in which we are involved, sometimes as initiators and sometimes as recipients. We can play the game in many ways, but the one thing God does not allow is that we observe from the sidelines. Like it or not, we're in it. And sooner or later we are in for it.

Here are the five story lines of Scripture. Refer to the chart, and you will see the specific texts and passages selected for each week. These are chosen to be either the most familiar or among the most representative or provocative passages from the books of the Old or New Testaments that are covered under the theme.

Israel's Covenant
Weeks 19-27
Approximately May through June

The Scriptures include Genesis, Exodus, Numbers, Deuteronomy, Judges, and Joshua. The story line follows the covenant that began with creation, and was broken (metaphorically or literally, as any given church wishes to interpret it) with the fall of Adam and Eve. The theme continues to explore the covenant with Noah, Abraham and Sarah, Israel and his descendants, and Moses. The patterns of promise, grace, sin, repentance, and forgiveness are explored—and the struggle of obedience, moral living, loyalty, and the victory of goodness are interpreted. The mentoring focus is on human yearning, marred by selfishness, and divine compassion, tempered by impatience. In Christian perspective, it anticipates Christ as the ultimate hope for a covenant fulfilled.

David's Legacy
Weeks 28-37
Approximately July through Mid-September

The Scriptures include Ruth, 1 and 2 Samuel, 1 and 2 Kings, 1 and 2 Chronicles, and the Psalms. The story line follows the historical and theological significance of David and his descendants, the struggle of the divided kingdom, and the call to repentance and faithfulness by the earliest prophets. David is both historic person and symbol of greatness, limitation, and forgiveness. In Christian perspective, this theme connects past experience and future promise through Christ.

Faithful Servants
Weeks 38-46
Approximately Mid-September through Mid-November

The Scriptures include Job, Nehemiah, Ecclesiastes, and the greater and lesser prophets. The story line follows the lives and teachings of key leaders obedient to God's will, who were in confrontation with political and social forces, and who guided the covenant community painfully and joyfully to be faithful to the ancient covenant. This theme explores issues of moral behavior, good and evil, judgment and reconciliation, despair and hope. In Christian perspective, this theme not only anticipates the coming of Christ, but also his moral teaching, prophetic witness, and mentoring for the spiritual life.

Jesus' Purpose
Weeks 47-52
Approximately Late November through January

The Scriptures include the Four Gospels and some reference to the Epistles. The story line follows the life, teaching, and significance of Jesus Christ. Various perspectives on the person and work of Jesus can be found in the New Testament itself, and this theme invites people to explore ancient and contemporary interpretations. The focus is less on Jesus' personal history, as on his meaning for salvation history. The preaching period does extend through the end of January, so that Christ's birth, life, death, and resurrection can be explored as a single story line with its own internal continuity.

Christians' Mission
Weeks 7-18
Approximately February through April

The Scriptures include the Acts of the Apostles, Epistles, and Revelation. The theme is titled in order to highlight both the corporate mission of the church, and the personal mission of every Christian—to follow Christ. It assumes that salvation history continues to unfold today as the good news is understood, shared, and experienced by all the cultures on earth. The theme explores the struggles of Christian mission, successes and failures of the church, advice for Christian living, and the hope of the future. Just as the theme of "Jesus' Purpose" connects with promise of "David's Legacy" and the example of "Faithful Servants," so also this theme for "Christians' Mission" connects with "Israel's Covenant" and the return of the world to grace.

As you study the chart, you will see how the theme is nuanced for meditation by the worship design team and for study by small groups. The Scriptures for the worship design team are intentionally chosen as counterpoint to those of the worship theme. The first three Old

Testament story lines all have the worship design team meditating on relevant passages from the *New Testament*. The last two New Testament story lines all have the team meditating on relevant passages from the *Old Testament*. Meanwhile, the small-group study texts all match the Scriptures chosen for worship, and take disciples deeper into understanding the Scriptures and overall theme. There are many Bible study resources that can be adapted by small-group leaders to the individual story lines, and small-group leaders can feel free to choose whatever works best with their particular group.

Old Trinity Church

As John pondered the strategy of the Disciple Cycle, the differences between it and the Common Lectionary became ever clearer. He realized that the originators of the Common Lectionary had also conceived it to be a kind of "disciple making and growing" process. The problem was that, as disciple-making processes go, cultural change and the demise of Christendom had rendered it less effective than it was intended to be. Among other things:

- *It assumed too much about the foundations of Bible awareness.*
- *It relied too heavily on distant experts to develop the preaching plan.*
- *It was too unresponsive to the flow of the calendar year.*
- *It was too intricate, abstract, and rigid in its presentation of Sunday texts.*
- *It presented fragments of stories, but not a story.*

John also knew that the Common Lectionary was designed to interface with a global, national, and regional church community that simply did not exist anymore. Most people simply would not move from the Seeker Cycle into the Common Lectionary–based worship service.

Old Trinity Church was blessed with a considerable number of retired clergy among the membership, and even a smattering of retired seminary professors, teachers, and assorted Ph.Ds. John thought it wise to make one of his many focus groups a gathering of these kinds of people. Their conversation was fairly amiable from the start, because acrimony over the very idea of adding mission-driven options for worship had already been overcome in planning the Seeker Cycle. These leaders all understood that worship was mission, and that being in mission was the worship most pleasing to God. Still, they had reservations.

"John, you say that the Disciple Cycle is a comprehensive reading of the Bible over a period of a year. But I looked at the texts used, and notice there are some books that are not even mentioned. Judges, Daniel, Leviticus, 1 and 2 Chronicles are some, and several epistles are not included. How can that be a comprehensive reading?"

"I never said it was a comprehensive reading," John replied. "I said it was a comprehensive study. These books can all be investigated as the worship team plans each story line, and as small groups go deeper into the books within each story line. Remember, both the worship team and small groups can customize the textual focus within each story line as the spirit leads. But the framework of the story line helps keep them on target and rescues them from whimsical tangents."

"But, John," interrupted George, one of his more conservative retired pastors, "the Bible says that 'all scripture is important to read' and you have clearly selected only certain texts for worship and small-group study—and these texts never seem to change from year to year. Some pieces of the Bible may never be studied unless expert leaders literally force people to look at them."

"Well," John said, "my memory is that all Scripture is 'profitable for teaching' specifically so that God's servants can be 'equipped for good work.' Let's be realistic, George. All Scripture may be profitable, but some are more profitable than others. And the measure of how 'profitable' it is has more to do with what good works follow rather than what historical or theological nuances can be explained."

"OK," George replied, "but what makes you think local church clergy and volunteers are better able to determine that than the experts at the seminary and the head office?"

"George," John replied, "haven't you been listening to the feedback in our church? The question people are asking is, 'What makes us think the experts and the seminary and head office are better able to decide what is profitable for any given microculture to read?' This is a fragmented world. The people who know best what they need are probably the people who are in the midst of the struggle."

"So the experts aren't necessary?" asked a retired seminary professor wryly. The twinkle in his eye suggested he expected, and agreed with, the coming answer.

"Not unnecessary," said John, "just secondary. The experts and the seminary and head office provide great resources, insights, and a framework to think. Where do you suppose the five story lines came from? But it is the local leaders in the context who need to write their own lectionary."

"*Speaking of the story lines,*" *contributed another focus group member,* "*why these story lines, and not others? I mean, there are other prolonged story lines of the Bible. For example, a Marxist reading of Scripture could argue that the economic and political liberation of the oppressed is a major story line. Or a gnostic or contemporary fundamentalist could argue that the dualistic struggle between good and evil is a major story line. Why these five? Is that just your middle-of-the-road, personal judgment?*"

"*No,*" *John replied, suddenly very self-conscious about his unfashionable glasses and expensive cardigan sweater his wife had given him for his fifty-fifth birthday.* "*The five story lines are borrowed from the perspective of the historic church. They would make perfect sense to Ignatius, Augustine, Saint Francis, Martin Luther, or John Wesley. They do not rule out discussion about any of those other themes you named, but they do not limit discussion to those themes either. More than this, those story lines reflect the perspective of the ancient Christians described in the New Testament itself. They viewed God's covenant, the significance of David, and the witness of the prophets and wise men—*"

"*And wise women!*" *interjected a retired university professor, remembering Deborah, Esther, Lydia, and the feminine metaphor for Wisdom in the book of Proverbs.*

"*And wise women,*" *added John hastily.* "*The ancients valued the Old Testament for precisely these story lines. Of course they valued the story line about Jesus. And they were particularly urgent to apply all of this to the pursuit of God's future mission in history. I admit that the five story lines are not tidily followed in the layout of biblical books as we have them today, but they are pretty faithful to the way early Christians made sense of their past, present, and future.*"

One retired pastor had been silent for all this time. "*John,*" *he said,* "*I can follow your reasoning regarding the story lines, and I can see both the focus and the flexibility you are giving to the small groups to follow up on the worship theme. But what is the rationale for juxtaposing lessons from the Old and New Testaments for the meditation of the worship design team?*"

"*It's an additional way to bring unity to the study of Scripture, and to introduce dialogue between the testaments. The idea is that the Old Testament story lines find the worship design team meditating on New Testament texts, and the New Testament story lines find the team meditating on Old Testament texts. The texts for meditation have been chosen because they are directly relevant, and in some cases refer to the texts for the worship theme.*"

Another silent member of the focus group spoke. "John, the plan sounds fine. You know I would do anything to get more people deeper into the faith and active in mission. But, John! Will it work? I mean, will people actually increase their worship attendance to do this, and discipline themselves to participate in a small group every week? Look at our adult Sunday school classes—they're pretty poorly attended and mostly older people. Do people have the will to do this? And if they have the will, do they have the time?"

John realized that this issue was their deepest source of skepticism. Many of the people in that room had tried to teach Sunday school and draw people into serious study of Scripture, and felt ambiguous about the results at best.

John said, "First, the Disciple Cycle is not aimed at people. It is aimed at leaders or people who want to become, or who feel called to become, leaders of the church. That is why the Disciple Cycle is so strict about requiring leaders to attend as a condition of their service, and expecting worship participants to participate in small groups. I am sure there will be exceptions, but we need to raise the bar on what is normative for church leadership. If church leaders model spiritual discipline, others will follow. Second, we are discovering in the Seeker Cycle that people are asking for more. There is a hunger for faith and hope, and there is a readiness to adjust to healthier and more spiritual lifestyles. Sure, 'normal' church members who attend the Common Lectionary–based service do not seem to have that hunger and desire, but I think they are the exceptions and not the rule in society today. If we do it right, present it right, and persist, I think the Disciple Cycle will succeed. Remember, nobody expects the Disciple Cycle worship service to be huge. If we just had fifty regular participants in the Disciple Cycle, that's fifty leaders of the church out of 500 worship participants in all of the other options— imagine what impact that could have on our mission!"

The Spiritual Life Focus

The Disciple Cycle is intended to have a very practical, and not merely intellectual, impact on worship participants. Now the model becomes even more clearly indebted to the monastic movement of the earliest church, because the goal is to shape the way we live and not just the way we think. For this reason, the worship design team will target each worship experience toward faith, hope, or lifestyle. No doubt some biblical passages touch on all three aspects of spiritual life, but more often than not there is one aspect that is most essential to the application of a biblical text.

Targeting worship toward faith means that the primary goal of the service is to help participants go deeper, and more clearly, into the convictions that give them strength, identity, and discernment. Faith is an experience of grace, a discipline of reflection, and a knowledge of truth. It is all of these things at once:

- Worship creates an environment or an opportunity for the Holy Spirit to impart conviction, certainty, or clarity to the individual. God erases doubts and skepticism, and instills in the heart of the believer a deeper confidence in his or her relationship to Christ.

- Worship invites participants into a process or discipline of reflection that involves listening and dialogue, analysis and synthesis, rational inquiry and mystical meditation. God guides people to understand their convictions, and coaches Christians to articulate their relationship to Christ.

- Worship teaches participants the real facts of their heritage, and historic and contemporary perspectives on life, death, God, sin, and salvation. It helps them understand the meaning behind the words, the reality behind the symbols, and the import behind the sacraments as they enlarge the experience of Christ.

Some worship services are clearly about faith. The worship design team will shape worship around the biblical passage to help people explore the principles and nuances of Christian faith. Worship strives to answer the question, *Why?*

Targeting worship toward hope means that the primary goal of the service is to help participants endure, persist, and anticipate God's grace, find encouragement for tomorrow, and discern the hidden purposes of God. Not only do Christians experience all the conflicts, disappointments, and tragedies of life that everyone else may experience, but they will also endure persecution, exploitation, career limitations, and belittlement because of their faith.

In the place where I live, a drunk driver killed a twenty-year-old young man. This is a tragic, but unfortunately all too common, experience. Almost two years later the drunk driver was sentenced to jail, and our local newspaper interviewed the mother of the victim. She gave the following statement:

> Twenty years of heaven on earth. From the time [my son] was born until his untimely death. Then came 488 days of hell on earth that you

just can't imagine . . . 488 days and never ending grief, pain, sorrow, crying, sadness, stress, devastation, anxiety, loneliness, emptiness, blackness, horror, torture, tears, hopelessness, tragedy, suffering, catastrophe, disbelief, nightmarish life, and uselessness. This cannot be my life now. But it's real. I have to take it. How much do I have to endure? How long? (*Guelph Mercury,* Saturday, Nov. 27, 2004)

This woman is probably a Christian, or at least a past or current member of a church. She may even be a member of a church board, a trustee, or a Sunday school teacher. In the face of such tragedy, she yearns for real hope.

Christian leaders lead, not just because of their great faith, but because of their ability to persist. They can overcome tragedy, stop crying, start smiling, live with joy, and continue in God's mission. That is the hope many of the prophets and apostles wanted to impart to their followers. That is a distinct focus of worship.

Targeting worship toward lifestyle may surprise traditional church members. Normally, the triad of words is "faith, hope, *and love.*" The substitution is quite intentional, and is again grounded in the historic experience of the church. In ancient times, love was not an emotion or a sentiment, but a lifestyle or pattern of behavior that was explicitly and even sacrificially benevolent toward other people. The substitution of terms in the Disciple Cycle is intended to focus Christians away from sentimentality toward behavioral modification.

Many of the biblical passages of the Disciple Cycle are about reshaping daily habits to reflect obedience to God's will (as in Old Testament story lines) or the fruits of the Spirit (as in New Testament story lines). Although this is about morality, ethical standpoints, and public policy, it is more than this. It is about spontaneous and daring behavior. It is about how Christians behave at work and at leisure; with work associates, family members, friends, neighbors, and strangers. It is about how Christians integrate all their activities in any twenty-four-hour period in a manner that is healthy, faithful, and missional.

The worship design team must decide in advance whether any given weekly worship service will be aimed at faith, hope, or lifestyle. This further focus helps all of the other teams prepare for the worship service. Note that these are not automatically assigned by the Disciple Cycle to any given biblical passage or weekly worship service. This is partly because the biblical texts are broad, and the focus this year may be different than next. And partly this is because the worship design team shapes worship out of its dialogue between the chosen biblical passage and their own observations and experiences of culture. Most of all, the determination of whether a biblical passage and worship service target faith, hope, or lifestyle will be made in dialogue between the worship design team and the small-group leaders. These small-group leaders help the worship design team discern what help will be key to the ongoing spiritual growth of the participants *at this time.*

It is here that the conversation between worship planners and small-group leaders is most important. The relationship between worship and small-group experience is not just one way. Worship sends people into small groups to explore the Scripture more deeply, but small-group leaders help the worship planner focus on what will be most productive or helpful to mature the Christian in the small group.

Old Trinity Church

It made sense to John that he would gain the feedback of his small-group leaders in developing the Disciple Cycle. Old Trinity Church had taken something of a shotgun approach to small-group ministry. Small groups were an eclectic bunch of age-based (youth, seniors), gender-based (men, women), and life-cycle-based (singles, widows, young couples) groups, along with some curriculum-based Bible studies, book clubs, and mission study groups. None of them were really that intentional about coaching spiritual life, and the church provided minimal training for their leaders. Group leaders were generally excited about the potential of the Disciple Cycle, but nervous about their skills and abilities to maintain a quality program.

Since the associate pastor, Maria, had been most involved with the various small groups of the church, she responded to the questions of this focus group. John listened carefully, because he frankly had little experience with serious spiritual growth through small groups and was afraid he might inadvertently cripple the Disciple Cycle.

"Is there a common curriculum or study guide around which every small group that spins out of the Disciple Cycle worship can be oriented?" asked one leader.

"Yes and no," Maria replied. "Certainly there are more and more discussion guides and commentaries emerging for the Bible passages of the Uncommon

Lectionary, but the real key to success is not finding a curriculum everybody can use, but training our small-group leaders to a uniform standard of quality. If we can train our leaders well, they can be free to choose whatever resources best help their small group. No single curriculum works for everybody—and more and more people learn best without a set curriculum."

"So what is the standard of quality to which leaders need to be trained?"

"There are many small-group strategies to consider, and we should look at as many as we can and customize something just right for ourselves. But my experience suggests that we need to train small-group leaders for at least the following:

- *Familiarity with the Disciple Cycle story lines*
- *Familiarity with the core values, beliefs, vision, and mission of the church*
- *Ability to articulate their own experience with Jesus*
- *Ability to mentor members of the group to discern personal mission*
- *Desire to lead the way to shape lifestyle around Christian faith and hope*

"I'm sure we can provide training to use various kinds of resources, but I think the most important thing is not to lose sight of the goal to grow and empower real disciples of Christ."

"Right now most of our groups just keep going as long as their members wish. Yet the Disciple Cycle is repeated every year. Are the small groups only in place for a year?"

"It would be nice if small-group life was orderly and predictable, but I think people will join and leave groups at many times during the year. We should probably say that our small groups will last a full year and only a year, but recognize that groups will be formed and be closed at any time. People will join the Disciple Cycle worship at any point in the year, and be encouraged to complete the cycle to the point where they began. Of course, we hope many will keep signing up for the worship and small-group experience year after year. The specific focus of worship and discussion will rarely be the same two years in a row."

"How many groups do you think we will need each year? And who is going to lead them?"

Maria laughed. "My crystal ball only tells me that we may well start by having more groups than we need—and end up with more people than we have groups. But consider this: If we just had fifty participants in the Disciple Cycle of worship out of a total of 500 in the other three services, we would only need about five groups (assuming five to twelve people in each group). Some leaders would clearly be from among the participants in the service. Some of you might want to be trained to lead a small group. Or you might know of others who would be excited about it. In the future, we hope the very success of growing disciples will generate more group leaders."

"You know," remarked one of the younger members of the focus group, "I'm excited and interested about leading such a group—and I would welcome whatever training you could give—but I'm afraid it would prove to be a lonely and intimidating task for fifty-two weeks each year."

"You're right," replied Maria, "and I appreciate both the honesty and integrity that are behind your remark. That's why I myself am going to lead a small group specifically for small-group leaders. It will not only be a source of ongoing training for each group leader in the Disciple Cycle, but it will allow us all to mutually support and advise one another as we work with our groups. I know everybody is busy, but I'm prepared to consider any option. We could even meet for breakfast at that great restaurant early every Sunday morning and arrange for a regular table."

The Christ Experience

The missional focus of the Uncommon Lectionary demands that it be centered on the person and work of Jesus Christ. Christology is the pivot on which the lectionary turns. The Disciple Cycle in particular does not try to present a systematic theology, or support particular theological traditions or perspectives, but it helps disciples focus and interpret their experience of Jesus.

Therefore, as the worship design team prepares for each worship service, it must answer the following questions:

- Into what experience of Christ is this Bible passage introducing us?
- What manner of Jesus is likely to encounter us in worship today?

The person of Jesus can be experienced in many different ways, by different cultures, at different times in an individual's life, with diverse results. The salvation of Christ can also be experienced in different ways, at different times, and in different life situations. The person of Jesus and the work of Jesus, the identity of Christ and the saving work of Christ, go together.

The fundamental orientation of the Disciple Cycle is the ancient Chalcedon Confession that the Christ is fully human and fully divine, that this is a paradox that ultimately can never be explained or proved, and that this paradoxical truth is crucial to salvation. In a sense, the salvation history that is the Bible is itself a nonstop paradox of how the infinite God can be available to the finite world, and why an infinite God who has everything should care the slightest amount for human beings who have nothing. The issue of incarnation—its fragile possibility and profound significance—threads its way throughout salvation history and is revealed most clearly and profoundly in Jesus.

Ancient Christians were not particularly systematic or uniform in their understanding of the person and work of Jesus. Systematic theology would come later, a gift of Christendom in the second millennium of the Christian era. In the first millennium (and in this emerging third millennium), Christology is the primary concern. Who is Jesus? And why should he matter to my microculture? That is the question seekers ask and disciples must answer.

The earliest disciples answered this question with a number of distinct perspectives and metaphors. The worship design team can use these biblical images and metaphors to focus each worship service. The clues to which image or metaphor of Christ is most relevant will be revealed from the biblical passages that are the focus of team meditation, worship theme, and small-group study. The following list is not complete, and worship design teams will be adding to it as they work:

- *Jesus the eternal, creative Word.* Jesus is the both the creative breath of God bringing all things into existence, and the underlying logic or structure of reason and life. (Genesis 1, Psalms 33 and 147, Isaiah 55, John 1.)
- *Jesus the Healer.* Jesus restores life to the dying, wellness to the sick, hope to the despairing. Jesus heals people physically, relationally, mentally, emotionally, and spiritually. (The miracles of Elijah and Elisha, Job 19:25, the many healings of the Gospels.)
- *Jesus the Shepherd.* Jesus is the leader, protector, and nurturer of the flock. He calls and his people hear his voice. Jesus stands with his people in times of trouble and distress. (Psalm 23, Ezekiel 34, Micah 7, John 10.)
- *Jesus the Door to Abundant Life.* Jesus is the way to truth and life, the guardian that wards off evil and provides access to grace for the good. He is the narrow path to salvation, or the one who

knocks on the door of your heart. (Matthew 7:13, John 10, Revelation 3.)

- *Jesus the True Vine.* Jesus is the living organism or vine, into which individuals can be grafted to receive the life-giving sap of God's grace, and bear fruit for God's mission. (John 15.)
- *Jesus the Moral Model.* Jesus is the paradigm for ethical advocacy and moral living, a liberator to the oppressed and vindicator of those who have been abused. (Amos 5; Psalms 10, 31, 72; Gospel of Mark.)
- *Jesus the Rabbinic Teacher.* Jesus is the wise teacher, one who interprets God's will and reveals the purpose of life, the spiritual guide through the ambiguities of life. (Proverbs, Psalms, Matthew 5–7.)
- *Jesus the Victorious King.* Jesus is the Messiah, the new David, the one who triumphs over evil, the leader who will return to vanquish hell and evil forces. (Daniel, Matthew 21, Revelation.)
- *Jesus the High Priest and Sacrificial Lamb.* Jesus is the sacrificial lamb, who takes his own life for the sake of the people. He stands between God and the people as intermediary. (Genesis 22, Exodus 12, Isaiah 53, John 1:29, 1 Corinthians 5:7, Hebrews, 1 Peter 1.)
- *Jesus the New Adam.* Jesus is the "true man," the only person without sin, who returns humanity and creation to the original perfection of Eden. Jesus heals the alienation between God and humanity. (Romans 5, 1 Corinthians 15.)
- *Jesus the Reconciler.* Jesus brings peace between peoples and between God and humanity. He restores the relationship of love between enemies, and bridges the gulf between God and the world. (2 Corinthians 5:19, Ephesians 2, Colossians 1.)

These are only some of the many metaphors or images of Christ that speak both to the mystery of his identity and the power of his work. Every worship service in the Disciple Cycle should identify some central image or metaphor for Christ that is particularly relevant to the Scripture and theme for that day. The same image or metaphor can be further discussed in the small group, as individuals begin to describe their own experience of Jesus that shapes faith, hope, and lifestyle.

Old Trinity Church

Old Trinity Church enjoyed a very healthy relationship with other churches in the city, and John participated regularly in the citywide ministerial. He invited his colleagues to offer feedback to the development of the Disciple Cycle of the Uncommon Lectionary. He assumed that this focus group would be the easiest and most supportive of all the groups—and was surprised to find that it was the most critical and skeptical.

His first surprise came with all the objections and reservations about the Christocentric nature of the Disciple Cycle. It was too vague; it was too specific. It was too judgmental; it was not dogmatic enough.

- *The liberals in the group worried that talking about Jesus would sound exclusive to minorities, other cultures, other religions, women, the poor, and anyone who was not a white Anglo-European. This puzzled John, because Old Trinity's experience with the Seeker Cycle was that minorities, people of other cultures and religions, women, the poor, and many others across the demographic diversity of the zip code were actually quite interested in, and unintimidated by, conversation about Christ. In fact, the people who seemed least interested were white Anglo-Europeans.*

- *The conservatives in the group worried that focusing on the* experience *of Christ, rather than rational doctrines about Christ, would water down the gospel and open the door to untold heresies. This puzzled John, because Old Trinity's experience so far was that the simple experience of Christ, in whatever way that was most meaningful to people, actually sharpened the gospel and reduced spiritual dilettantism.*

John began to sense that most of his colleagues were preoccupied with defending a particular agenda or defining themselves by what they were not rather than by what they were.

"If a church does not focus on Christ, then what exactly is the church about? Many philanthropic organizations can do what we do cheaper and more effectively. How can we celebrate the sacraments, repeat the creeds, and observe the historic liturgies and not believe what we are saying? If we practice one thing in worship, but cast doubt on the centrality of Christ in private, is that not hypocrisy? And the seekers we work with at Old Trinity are not stupid—they can sniff out hypocrisy in an instant."

John said this aloud—and many of his liberal colleagues suggested he was a dangerous fundamentalist.

"If we reduce the experience of Christ to rational formulas to which people must simply give assent, then what exactly happens to the infinite mystery and relevance of Jesus who can encounter unique individuals with grace in

countless ways? How can Christ touch the real diversity of humanity, trans-form lives, and reshape society, with apocalyptic power, if we try to keep grace bound up in a little, rational, dogmatic formula? If we preach the power of grace in public, but limit access to grace in private, is that not hypocrisy? All those seekers who embrace, and are embraced by, the fullness of God aren't about to allow themselves to be locked up again in a tidy, rational, box of doctrinal uniformity."

John said this aloud—and many of his conservative colleagues suggested he was a dangerous libertarian.

John was also surprised that his colleagues were so antagonistic about the distinct tracks of worship planning and the important role of the worship design team. At first it seemed there was just a simple misunderstanding. Many clergy were just too exhausted preparing the single, traditional, Common Lectionary–based worship service. The thought of planning and leading two very distinct services, with different Scriptures, and distinctly customized sermons, for specific mission results just overwhelmed them. John patiently explained that other staff and volunteer laity would be taking leadership in planning and leading worship—even in preaching—and that it was not all dependent on the clergy.

However, that opened the door for more anxieties about the quality and integrity of laity in planning and leading worship. John had always heard his colleagues extol the leadership roles of laity, so this took him aback. It became apparent that the real issue for many of his colleagues was not that they couldn't do this kind of worship, but that they must be at the center of all worship. Clergy colleagues might complain about the burden of planning and leading worship, but still believed it was their duty and privilege to bear that burden alone.

In a moment of insight, John realized his colleagues were only voicing his own hidden anxieties and needs. He, too, would find it hard to let go, and allow his worship teams real power to discern, design, implement, and evaluate the alternative cycles of worship. Yes, he would have to work hard to ensure the quality and integrity of worship through mentoring and coaching, but there was still that fundamental leap he would have to make to really transfer authority to the laity. He would have to let them struggle, experiment, fail, learn, and grow. In the long run he knew that would build better, deeper, more powerful worship, but like a parent allowing his children to walk he would have to resist the temptation to intervene and take control.

John had gone to the ministerial with the hope of finding other church partners who might work with Old Trinity Church in this new direction of worship planning. This was a partial success. He found there were two kinds of clergy in his citywide ministerial, and they were not defined by theology, ideology, denomination, or even attitudes toward worship.

- *The first group of clergy shook his hand and said, "Good luck—we'll pray for you!" Yet John could see they were profoundly cynical. In their hearts, they were convinced it wouldn't work. Indeed, John suspected they believe nothing would work. People in the city were not interested, would not get involved, would never accept such discipline, and would not come. The temptations were too great, the conspiracy of alienation from the church was too powerful, and the best the declining churches could hope for was maintain a righteous remnant who could pay Christian professionals to do God's work.*
- *The second group of clergy shook his hand and said, "Let's have lunch! We want to work with you!" They may not be sure about every aspect of the plan, but they had hope and were willing to customize. In their hearts, they were convinced it would work. People really were interested, many would get involved, lay leaders would undertake such discipline, and the public would respond. The yearning was too great, the visible demonstration of God's grace was too powerful, and the best faithful churches should hope for was to bring seekers in, grow disciples up, and send apostles out.*

Old Trinity Church began to forge a new network that day. The people who joined tended to be new communities of faith and non-Anglo-European communities of faith (Hispanic, African, Asian, and every microculture you could name). They tended to be small churches that were one step from closure and had nothing to lose, and big churches with lots of human resources that lacked only a compelling vision. Some were liberal. Some were conservative. All of them had a tremendous desire to go deeper and leap farther in God's mission.

CHAPTER SIX

Getting
Organized

M ost clergy establish a routine for worship and sermon preparation. It is the only way they can provide quality spiritual direction for worship in the midst of very busy lives. The challenge is to make this routine a spiritual discipline, and not simply a repetitive task. The ability to infuse that routine with prayer, personal reflection on Scripture, spirited conversations with church members and complete strangers, and intentional outreach to people for whom one's heart bursts with compassion, makes all the difference between a slide into burnout and a path to grace.

The Uncommon Lectionary is particularly insistent that clergy and lay leaders make their worship and sermon preparation routines a spiritual discipline. The Seeker Cycle simply will not work unless pastor and worship team have ignited a heartburst for people beyond the church membership through deep prayer and conversation with culture. The Disciple Cycle simply will not work unless pastor and worship team have equipped themselves to be mentors for future disciples. Task-driven routines encourage leaders to play it safe, reduce risks, and be predictable. Spiritual discipline encourages leaders to explore new possibilities, take risks, and expect the unpredictable. If worship really is about creating opportunities for God and humanity to connect, then the only sure thing is that nothing is certain. The ability of a pastor or lay leader to come before God in worship, not as a professional, but as a model of the spiritual life, is the authenticity for which seekers and disciples yearn.

Clergy usually spend time in July or August reviewing lectionary texts for the coming year, gathering resources, consulting with organists or music directors, meeting with Christian education staff and curriculum planners, and identifying major celebrations. Occasionally, they may retreat with other staff or lay leaders in January, specifically to prepare for Lent and Easter. These planning sessions allow musicians, teachers, hospitality teams, newsletter editors, and everyone else to focus their future rehearsals, classroom schedules, refreshments, and publicity.

Clergy establish a weekly routine to refine the details of next Sunday's service and sermon. Monday or Tuesday they review the lectionary texts, pray for guidance, and choose or write appropriate prayers, children's stories, hymns, and so on. These are duly passed on to organists and worship leaders. In a large church, there may be a meeting with staff involved in worship. In a small church, the choir is informed of the hymns before the rehearsal on Thursday night. Some clergy will be a part of a lectionary discussion group with clergy colleagues that meets later in the week. The sermon is written Friday or Saturday. The extent to which the sermon is influenced by conversations or experiences within the church membership or within the larger mission field varies a great deal from one week to the next.

The value of a lectionary is that clergy begin the weekly routine with a text that is relevant to a time line, a context, a plan for Bible study, and a larger congregational mission. In using the Common Lectionary, clergy begin with a set of four brief texts (Old Testament, Psalm, Epistle, and Gospel). These are relevant to the Christian year, the global Christendom context, a focus on Bible study oriented to a theological or ideological thread uniting the four texts, and the programs of the church that require personal and financial support. In using the Uncommon Lectionary, clergy begin with a single extended passage of Scripture for worship, supported by Scriptures to guide personal or team meditation and small-group discussion. This single extended Scripture is relevant to the spiritual moments and flow of experience in the public calendar, the actual demographic diversity of the church's primary mission field, a plan to learn the basic texts or story lines of the Bible, and the congregational mission to reach out to strangers that require personal and financial support.

The spiritual routine to plan and implement the Uncommon Lectionary will vary from leader to leader and, because of the contextual nature of the plan, is even more open to customization than other lectionary patterns.

The Seeker Cycle

The routine development of the Seeker Cycle will look something like this. The number of people involved, and the complexity of worship planning and leadership, will of course vary according to the size of the church. More significantly, the format and style of worship will change over time depending on the mission target and mission purpose of worship.

Annual Planning Retreat: July or August

Pastors will handpick the members of the worship design team. (If the custom of the church is to elect these individuals, the pastor will prepare the nominations slate.) This ensures that the worship design team includes key roles for shaping the message, coordinating appropriate music, and developing interactive processes (liturgy, drama, dance, images, sound effects, decorations, and anything that creates an environment for God and people to connect).

The retreat includes members of the worship design team and any key leaders they invite to join them. This could include guests from microcultures within the primary mission field for whom the church has a particular heartburst. It might also include community leaders familiar with the demographic trends of the primary mission field. During the retreat:

1. Participants review the core values, beliefs, vision, and mission of the church, and spend time in extended prayer for those people or microcultures who are strangers to grace, and for whom their hearts burst in desire to help them experience grace.
2. Participants review demographic and lifestyle trends in their primary mission field. The primary mission field is defined by the average travel time or distance people in their context are willing to drive to work or shop. There are currently as many as sixty identifiable lifestyle segments possible in any given mission field.

3. Participants review the Seeker Cycle chart and calendar. They customize and complete the spiritual calendar of the public, and refine the basic Bible texts that will be addressed in any given week.

4. Participants listen to the feedback of voices from the primary mission field and from the participants of past worship services from the previous year.

5. Participants tentatively refine the worship themes for each week, along with a key message or image that will help others focus their contributions to each worship service.

6. Participants tentatively define the mission purpose of each worship service (healing, coaching, celebration, cherishing, and so on).

7. Participants organize hospitality ministries both to welcome newcomers and to build relationships following the worship services.

8. Participants confirm ongoing methods for coordinating planning and sharing feedback (phone numbers, meeting schedules, e-mail addresses, and so on).

9. Participants duplicate the revised calendar for the Seeker Cycle. Make sure all leaders in the church have a copy of the calendar. Share an abbreviated version of the calendar in the advertising for the church to the public.

The planning retreat is only to identify target publics, major themes, worship formats, and key tasks. Since the Seeker Cycle worship services are intended to be very responsive to the emerging issues and concerns of the community, further detailed planning will happen on a weekly basis.

Seeker Cycle Begins January 1:
The Start of the Calendar Year

The normal pattern of church life at the beginning of the twenty-first century has been to focus the early months of the New Year on the aftermath of Christmas. This often involved explanations of Epiphany, doctrinal nuances of Christian faith, and special topics identified by denominational parents that might also be addressed in congregational annual meetings or oversight conferences. In other words, the worship experience following Christmas often turned inward to focus on the institutional needs of the church or the uniformity of Christendom. That pattern is being reversed.

The Seeker Cycle starts the New Year with the same preoccupation with fresh starts, new beginnings, and resolutions for future positive behavior that is on the minds of the general public. Therefore, the Scriptures begin with passages about creation, new creation, and expectations for faithful and healthy Christian behavior. The worship experience does not turn inward to focus on institutional needs, but turns outward to elaborate the significance of new life in Christ.

Issues and agendas that inform annual meetings and oversight conferences may still be addressed by the church, but *not* through the Seeker Cycle worship. These matters are neither part of the liturgy and preaching, nor even a part of the announcements and handouts. Seekers are never invited to management or oversight meetings. They are *always* invited into other forms of fellowship, small-group experience, or mentoring relationships.

The Weekly Routine

The worship design team should meet Monday or Tuesday of each week. In small churches this may be as few as three people. The message shaper may be the senior or assistant pastor, or very possibly a layperson who is a credible spiritual leader. It is not uncommon for this person to also be a musician who is part of a band or musical ensemble of some kind. The music coordinator may be an organist or traditional choir director, but more likely is a person familiar with various genres of music, with networks in the community including bands and semi-professional performers. The process developer may be a staff person, but often this is an entirely new position for a volunteer experienced in liturgy, drama, and interactive worship. It is important that no single person design worship. Worship is designed by a team.

The team meeting each week will follow a similar agenda to the original planning retreat. They will pray and meditate together, using the Scripture provided for team meditation; review the values, beliefs, vision, and mission of the church; review demographic and lifestyle trends in the primary mission field; and then plan the details of worship:

- Define the core message and central image of worship.
- Define the basic format or missional purpose of worship.
- Identify key tasks that various individuals or groups must undertake to prepare worship.

Since worship services will vary in purpose, format, and message, the leadership of worship may also change from week to week. The design team pays special attention to identifying and equipping leaders for worship.

Assuming that the pastor will be the speaker or preacher for the service, he or she will gather resources to prepare the message. This may involve a lectionary discussion group among peers using the Uncommon Lectionary or a focus group of people from the target microcultures that are the heartburst for the church. If English is the second language for any group, the design team will want to anticipate the need for translation.

The music coordinator will select the appropriate genre of music, select whatever groups or instrumentations are necessary, and equip choirs, bands, or other leaders for the worship service. The process developer will meet with technology teams to create computer graphics, or drama teams to write scripts, or children's ministry teams to develop stories, or decoration teams to create sanctuary symbols and environments, or sacrament teams to customize liturgy.

Immediately after the worship service, members of the worship design team will collect and communicate feedback to evaluate the success of their work. Success is measured in three ways:

- Has the worship helped strangers to grace experience God's grace intellectually, emotionally, or relationally? Are people better off for the worship experience?
- Has the worship helped participants experience Jesus Christ?
- Has the worship helped participants understand, appreciate, or apply this basic text of the Bible to their daily lives?

Evaluation should be done immediately after worship, so that the feedback can be reviewed by the worship design team as the weekly routine begins with their meeting on Monday or Tuesday.

Since worship in the Seeker Cycle is especially unpredictable, and intentionally open to the spontaneity of God and people, the design team spends more time discussing alternative scenarios and faithful responses to unexpected events. Issues of safety and confidentiality are repeatedly discussed, and plans for personal and prayer support are crucial.

The Disciple Cycle

The routine development of the Disciple Cycle will look something like this. The number of people involved, and the complexity of worship planning and leadership, will of course vary according to the size of the church.

Annual Planning Retreat: January or February

Pastors will handpick the members of the worship design team. This will almost certainly be a *different* team from the one that plans the Seeker Cycle. The core team still includes key roles for shaping the message, coordinating appropriate music, and developing interactive processes (liturgy, drama, dance, images, sound effects, decorations, and anything that creates an environment for God and people to connect). However, the core team may also include a coordinator for small groups.

The retreat includes members of the worship design team and any key leaders they invite to join them, plus small-group leaders who lead the postworship midweek groups. During the retreat:

1. Participants review the core values, beliefs, vision, and mission of the church, and spend time in extended prayer to seek God's guidance to grow disciples who will follow Christ into mission.
2. Participants review the Disciple Cycle chart and calendar, feeling free to add to it or refine it based on the experience of the previous years in their unique context of mission. Review the five story lines that will be followed during the year.
3. Participants review demographic and lifestyle trends in their primary mission field. The primary mission field is defined by the average travel time or distance people in their area are willing to drive to work or shop. There are currently as many as sixty identifiable lifestyle segments possible in any given mission field.

4. Participants listen to the feedback of small-group leaders, and discern the unique issues and questions that emerged from the past year.
5. Participants tentatively identify which worship services will be oriented to faith, hope, or lifestyle, and list the challenges, issues, questions, or concerns that will likely be most relevant given your understanding of the mission field and the current spiritual growth of the congregation.
6. Participants tentatively identify the experience of Jesus (a key metaphor, image, or conviction that will specifically connect people in worship with Christ) for each worship service. Note especially celebrations for Holy Communion or baptism as they might be observed in the context of your church or denominational practice.
7. Participants tentatively identify the key message to be communicated in each worship service, and the image or picture that captures the experience you hope participants will have in each worship service.
8. Participants confirm ongoing methods for consultation (phone numbers, meeting schedules, e-mail addresses, etc.), and methods to evaluate the success of each worship service.
9. Participants confirm methods for long-distance learning, including video and audio taping, Web site archiving and message boards, and other means to help participants engage the worship services with weekly consistency.
10. Participants duplicate the revised calendar for the Disciple Cycle. Make sure all leaders in the church have a copy of the calendar.

Disciple Cycle Begins Week 19: Mid or Late May

The normal pattern of church life at the beginning of the twenty-first century has been to wind down the program year of the church in anticipation of lower worship attendance and summer holidays. (In the Southern Hemisphere, summer holidays will occur in different dates, but the same winding down of the program year is typical.) This may still be the case for participants in the Seeker Cycle of the

Uncommon Lectionary, and for participants in an ongoing Common Lectionary service. However, this "normal" process is reversed with the Disciple Cycle.

Congregational leaders will be expected to create momentum that pumps up leaders for the Disciple Cycle of worship. Remember that leaders should be expected to participate in the Disciple Cycle as a condition for service in their office, and that staff will need to coordinate their own vacation times so that there is no vacuum of leadership for this worship alternative. In small churches, pastors may choose to take vacations at other times in the year when lay leaders are more readily available to continue the Disciple Cycle—or church leaders may need to be more intentional about avoiding mere "pulpit supply" and obtaining quality leadership to lead the Disciple Cycle.

This decision to pump up rather than wind down worship for the summer months of the calendar is one of the greatest challenges and strengths of the Disciple Cycle. It goes against the grain of what has become normative in the past fifty years of church life—but it recaptures the vitality of the church of previous centuries. It keeps leaders focused on mission and spiritually growth as individuals throughout the entire year. There should be no down time for congregational mission.

The Weekly Routine

The worship design team should meet Monday or Tuesday of each week. In small churches this may be as few as three people: the message shaper (pastor), music coordinator (organist), and process developer (drama coach). In larger churches, this may include team leaders from technology crews, hospitality teams, and small-group coordinators. The point is that the pastor should not develop worship alone, but in the spiritual context of a team that is clearly united in a common vision for the worship service.

The team meeting each week will follow a similar agenda to the original planning retreat. Team members will pray and meditate together, using the Scripture provided for team meditation; review the values, beliefs, vision, and mission of the church; listen to any feedback from small-group leaders and participants in worship; and then plan the details of worship:

- Define the orientation of worship to faith, hope, or lifestyle.
- Define the Christ center of worship.
- Define the key message to be communicated in word and image.

The team can then discuss various tactics for teaching, music, and process. Team members then leave the meeting to gather their own task groups to implement plans and improvise tactics later in the week. Assuming that the pastor will be the speaker or preacher for the service, he or she will gather resources to prepare the message. This may involve a lectionary discussion group among peers using the Uncommon Lectionary, or among small-group leaders to integrate the message with midweek study, or among discussion groups involving clergy and laity from within and beyond the church.

The music coordinator will select the appropriate genre of music, select whatever groups or instrumentations are necessary, and equip choirs, bands, or other leaders for the worship service. The process developer will meet with technology teams to create computer graphics, or drama teams to write scripts, or children's ministry teams to develop stories, or decoration teams to create sanctuary symbols and environments, or sacrament teams to customize liturgy.

Immediately after the worship service, members of the worship design team will collect and communicate feedback to evaluate the success of their work. Success is measured in three ways:

- Has the worship effectively communicated faith, or inspired hope, or shaped lifestyle for the participants?
- Has the worship helped participants experience Jesus Christ?
- Has the worship informed and enhanced small-group discussion during the week?

Evaluation should be done immediately after worship, so that the feedback can be reviewed by the worship design team as the weekly routine begins with their meeting on Monday or Tuesday.

As the worship and church grow, planning and implementation may well become more complex. The routine may shift to a two- or even three-week production schedule, rather than one week. This means that worship design teams are actually working on the development of the service two or three Sundays away, even as their various task groups are finalizing details for the coming service this week.

Old Trinity Church

Old Trinity Church has been using the Uncommon Lectionary for six years now. They started with the Seeker Cycle for two years, and then launched the Disciple Cycle in the third year. It took a while to experiment with various configurations of the worship design team, as people slowly learned new leadership roles. Old Trinity Church continues to have a Common Lectionary track of very traditional worship, with a separate planning team. Congregational staff, board, and core leaders today are very precise about the boundaries of their primary mission field, and very intentional about tracking demographic and lifestyle trends. Their expectations for spiritual growth and modeling leadership for staff and core lay leaders have risen considerably in the past five years.

A Week in the Life of the Seeker Cycle Worship Design Team

Pastor John's personal heartburst for despairing businesspeople and social service volunteers on the brink of suicide has been broadened and focused on blue collar and white collar members of the work force in the urban core. Because their context is experiencing significant growth in Hispanic or Latino communities, everything they do includes a Spanish-speaking component. The associate minister already speaks Spanish, and John has been taking Spanish lessons to preach fluently in a second language.

The worship design team meets Monday morning from 9:00 to 12:00, and eats lunch together in a nearby restaurant until 1:00. The team consists of John (senior pastor and message shaper), Maria (associate pastor and process developer), Alex (the volunteer bandleader and semiprofessional musician from the community), Nicole (health care professional and senior manager from a nearby hospital), and one or more volunteers from the Hispanic community who rotate their involvement on the team. The organist/choir director used to be on the team, but as the Seeker Cycle service focused, and the Disciple Cycle service began, the staff redeployed his energies to the other teams. Of course, he is totally supportive of the three options of worship.

This particular week the team is planning worship in recognition of May Day, which in this community has traditionally been a celebration of family life and baptism. The Seeker Cycle chart needs to be adjusted, because April only has four Sundays. The team decides to rearrange the worship theme texts for this Sunday and the next. They borrow the Mark 10:14 passage ("Let the little children come . . .") originally scheduled for next week, and couple it with the Isaiah 55:11 passage ("My word . . . shall not return to me empty . . .") for this week. That will leave the John text as originally scheduled for the worship theme next week.

Their core message is that God's word brings everlasting life, and they plan to fill the worship with images of water fountains. The central experience will be baptism, and they have about fifteen infants and children, and one adult, to baptize. About a third of the families involved have Spanish as their primary language.

The team develops instructions to various task groups about the images to be projected by computer on screens, and the symbols and decorations that will transform the gymnasium into a garden. Special attention will be given to reproducing the scents of flowers and handing out free tissues for people with allergies. (Sneezing will be recognized and celebrated as a sign of the movement of the Spirit.) There are two major adaptations to worship:

- *A huge central fountain and pool will be created on stage in the gymnasium. They will inflate a large swimming pool, decorate it appropriately to simulate a garden fountain, and spend part of their worship budget on the most powerful water pump and fountain they can buy from the home renovation box store. This will be illumined by colored lights. They will baptize people in groups, with entire families invited to take off their shoes, roll up their pants, and join the pastors in the pool to splash the kids with "holy water." (The trustees and custodians have already been alerted that there will be a mess). Maria, the process developer, will take care of the planning.*
- *The microphones will be routed through two computers that will be programmed with dictation software. One computer will automatically transcribe spoken words into English, and the other computer will automatically transcribe the same spoken words into Spanish. The software is anything but perfect, and the pastor will need to practice so that the computer recognizes his voice, but it will communicate the idea that "God's word does not return empty" and make many of the Spanish-speaking family guests feel at home.*

The planning team has decided that the mission purpose of this worship service is really about celebration. They expect that what will be most memorable and inspiring will not be the preaching, but the action, drama, images, and excitement of the children and families.

As the planning team meditates on the Scripture from Acts designated for this day (Philip baptizing the Ethiopian), they focus especially on the miraculous action of the Spirit implied in the story. The Spirit sweeps Philip away to a deserted road to meet a total stranger, miraculously makes available a pool of water on a desert road, and then sweeps Philip away again to another mission. "Sweep us away, Lord," they pray. "Sweep the people in this worship service away, into grace, into mission!" The team decides to give away to every person as he or she leaves the worship service a bottle of water with a street corner in their city written on it in permanent ink. They are going to ask people to go to that corner, remember this day of baptism, thank God, and pour it out on the sidewalk as a prayer to God. If anyone asks why, God will give them the words to speak at the time.

After the planning team meeting, the team members split up to fulfill their tasks and equip their own teams. The bandleader develops the music; the drama team develops a script; the technology team programs the computers; the fountain task force creates the special effect. The pastor meets with an Uncommon Lectionary study group to help develop his message. When he explains what the worship service will look like, they shake their heads in amazement, and pray for him anyway.

A Week in the Life of the Disciple Cycle Worship Design Team

Meanwhile, a totally different team is preparing the Disciple Cycle service for the same Sunday, the first Sunday in May. This is toward the completion of the third full cycle of this lectionary for Old Trinity Church, and by now the team has become used to the process.

This team actually meets on Tuesday afternoon, two weeks in advance of this particular worship service. They have learned that they need a two-week production schedule to prepare the kind of intensive, quality mentoring experience most valued by the participants. The team is actually smaller than the Seeker Cycle team, since each of the team members has his or her own task group to equip and guide. The message shaper for this team is a retired professional educator from a local community college. He may or may not be the actual preacher/speaker, but he will brief the senior pastor or lay leader as required. The organist/choir director is a part of this team, and the music will usually be classical or smooth jazz. The associate minister is now focused as a cell group developer, and she helps shape the process of each worship service. Finally, a leader of one of the postworship small groups joins the team on a rotating basis.

The May Day service is in fact week 18, and the last Sunday for the

130 — Introducing the Uncommon Lectionary

Disciple Cycle. The story line is "Christians' Mission," and the theme is "Eternal Hope and the End of Time."

The team began with extensive prayer and meditation, based on the texts from Jeremiah 31 and 33. The associate pastor was prepared to answer questions about the historical context and references of the passage. After silent prayer, the team shared the words or images that touched their hearts most powerfully. Jeremiah 31:11 leapt out for their attention: "For the LORD has ransomed Jacob, / and has redeemed him from hands too strong for him." Both the message and the image grasped their imaginations, and they were convinced the Holy Spirit was leading them to shape the worship service around this sign of hope.

The theme scripture for worship is 1 Thessalonians 4 and 5. The team realized that, although the central point of the epistle is to give suffering and anxious Christians hope, it was also coaching Christians how to persist in the spiritual life in the midst of temptations, and how to endure in the faith despite opposition. The sermon will study the following passage verse by verse:

> *For God has destined us not for wrath but for obtaining salvation through our Lord Jesus Christ, who died for us, so that whether we are awake or asleep we may live with him. Therefore encourage one another and build up each other, as indeed you are doing. But we appeal to you . . . to respect those who labor among you, and have charge of you in the Lord and admonish you; esteem them very highly in love because of their work. Be at peace among yourselves. And we urge you . . . to admonish the idlers, encourage the faint hearted, help the weak, be patient with all of them. See that none of you repays evil for evil, but always seek to do good to one another and to all. Rejoice always, pray without ceasing, give thanks in all circumstances; for this is the will of God in Christ Jesus for you. (1 Thess 5:9-18)*

Each verse will be presented in different ways—sometimes through traditional teaching, sometimes through video clip, and sometimes using music and images. As always, Bibles will be handed out, people will be encouraged to take notes, and questions will be welcome at any time. At Old Trinity Church, there are about fifty leaders in attendance, and most of them bring laptop computers on which there is software for many versions of the Bible.

What experiences of Christ, or what manner of Jesus, are people going to share in this service? The worship team pondered this issue with great care. It would be easy to allow the service to become so diffuse with tips and tactics to endure as to become pedantic. It would also be easy to allow the future small-group discussion of Romans and Revelation to become a debate between dogmatic speculations of the end time. The breakthrough came when the small-group coordinator pointed out these Scriptures in Romans 10 from the intended study of the small groups:

> *But the righteousness that comes from faith says, "Do not say in your heart, 'Who will ascend into heaven?' " (that is, to bring Christ down) "or 'Who will descend into the abyss?' " (that is, to bring Christ up from the dead). But what does it say? "The word is near you, / on your lips and in your heart" (that is, the word of faith that we proclaim); because if you confess with your lips that Jesus is Lord and believe in your heart that God raised him from the dead, you will be saved. (vv. 6-9)*

"The 'Cosmic Christ'!" said John. "That is the image we want people to have of Jesus. We want people to know that, no matter what happens, Jesus is Lord. Christ is victorious. Whether we wake or sleep, live or die, we are Christ's and held in God's grace." This image, of course, is an ancient Byzantine image. The team decided to purchase Byzantine icons of the Cosmic Christ from the resource center of the Greek Orthodox Church in the city, and give every worship participant an image to focus his or her prayer and mediation during the week and into his or her small-group discussion.

Lest this become too abstract and theoretical for some, the team decided to begin and end the service on a single dramatic theme. They were still seized by the image from Isaiah: The Lord redeems Jacob "from hands too strong for him." The opening drama of worship would depict a terrified man surrounded by a mob—hands grabbing and holding him in mayhem—rescued by Christ dressed in white and led to safety. The service would end with a surprise. The fifty worshipers would not be allowed to leave! They would arrange for a "gang" (the youth group gladly volunteered to dress up for the part!) to block the exits and hold people back. Christ would appear, and the "gang" would leave the doors open and carry Jesus away instead. The last words of the service will be from Jesus calling to the worshipers: "Go ahead," he shouts confidently, "I'll be fine!"

Later in the week, the small-group leaders reported via e-mail to the worship team. The discussions had been intense and emotional. One woman who had recently suffered the death of her husband, and who herself was wrestling with a chronic illness, declared tearfully and boldly her conviction that "whether we wake or whether we sleep we still live with him." She vowed to make that message the cornerstone of her leadership with the visitation teams of the church.

The Future of Old Trinity Church

Seven years later, the mission impact of Old Trinity Church across the city and in their primary mission field has increased exponentially. Their leaders are involved as helpers or board members in more social service and health care agencies than ever before. The suicide rate in the city may not be lower— but it is no higher, despite the deepening economic and social problems of their urban environment. The name of Old Trinity Church is on the lips of more residents, commuters, and community leaders than ever before. And yes, attendance in the Seeker Cycle has grown to about 300 on a good day in November, spiking to 500 on the bigger "holy days" of the public calendar. Attendance in the Disciple Cycle has increased to between 75 and 100. The expectation of attendance among officers and elected leaders of the church has begun to take hold, and board members and leaders from other churches have begun to attend following their own Sunday morning services! They are rapidly becoming known as a teaching church for missionaries across the city.

Pastor John notes with some pride that the Common Lectionary–based, traditional worship service has not only been revitalized, but it also has grown (about 200 on a good day in Lent and spiking to 350 for Easter and Christmas Day Eucharist).

"The leaders who have been trained and motivated through the Disciple Cycle are now planning and leading the Common Lectionary option of worship," John says with satisfaction. "I just do the preaching, and let them do the rest." The Common Lectionary service is intentionally being advertised to reach people in the suburbs, and itself has become an act of mission.

John is often questioned by other church leaders, "What happens to the Sunday school, larger groups, and fellowship events?"

"Our traditional men's and women's groups, adult Bible study classes, and many fellowship events aimed at our members still follow the Christian year and use (somewhat loosely) the Common Lectionary. But our children's Sunday school, youth group, cell groups, and board meetings follow the Uncommon Lectionary. Who knows how that will change over time?"

Perhaps the most exciting strategic initiative for Old Trinity Church is the founding of New Trinity Church at another site in the city. Yes, they are planting a church once again! But they have learned from previous mistakes, and are not trying to make New Trinity Church a clone of Old Trinity Church.

New Trinity Church is still a small church with limited resources. They decided to rotate the Seeker Cycle and Disciple Cycle worship options every other year. This year the one worship service will be Seeker Cycle, next year they will follow the Disciple Cycle, and so on. The same worship design team will handle both cycles, and they can rely on volunteers from Old Trinity Church to help them with images, drama, and other tactics. In this way, they hope to leverage the process of inviting seekers, maturing disciples who invite more seekers, who grow into more disciples, and so increase both the outreach and the leadership base of the church.

Eventually, they will separate the two cycles into distinct services of worship. Once New Trinity Church reaches a critical mass of 250 in Seeker Cycle worship and 30 in Disciple Cycle worship, they will add yet a third worship option: a Common Lectionary worship alternative! This strategic plan surprises many observers. They had always thought that John's hidden agenda was to eliminate the Common Lectionary–based, traditional service in favor of the cycles of the Uncommon Lectionary. But John just shakes his head and smiles.

"We never said the Common Lectionary–based, traditional worship was bad or irrelevant. We only recognized that it was intended to consolidate a membership, not reach out in mission. As soon as we returned worship to its ancient orientation of mission, the Common Lectionary–based service was revitalized and restored to its useful place in building up the body of Christ. That worship service makes a vital contribution to the life and mission of Old Trinity Church, and to any church that places itself clearly and solely in the path of God's mission."

CHAPTER SEVEN

Great Worship

When worship becomes an act of mission, it shifts from good to great. An act of mission is an act of God. It is the eternal act of God to redeem and reconcile the world, revealed in that microcosm of experience we call worship. By our very nature humanity is a stranger to grace, but yearns for God. By God's very nature, God is the giver of grace, stretching to embrace the world. Every worship service is a reenactment of that act of mission, and we are drawn into that act of mission. When worship becomes an act of mission, it ceases to be about us and becomes about God's mission. The challenge of worship is no longer to perfect it, refine it, universalize it, standardize it, and make it correct. The challenge of worship is to focus it on mission, open it to God's power, make universal God's love to include all the microcultures in the postal code, and grow disciples who will share that grace over and over again every day of the week. That's great worship. That's the kind of worship the spiritually yearning, institutionally alienated publics seek; that's the kind of worship faithful Christians desire; and that's the kind of worship God expects.

Worship as an act of mission includes two constantly reinforcing movements of the Spirit: mission and commission. Worship draws people in and sends them out. The people who are sent out, draw people in. The Seeker Cycle requires a Disciple Cycle; the Disciple Cycle results in a Seeker Cycle. If all you do is draw seekers into worship that transforms lives, without making them disciples, what is the value in that? If all you do is send out disciples to do good deeds without drawing them into worship, what is the value in that? Mission and commission go hand in hand. The one cannot survive without the other.

The purpose of the Common Lectionary is really membership consolidation. This is a good purpose! In the Christendom world, it had almost universal appeal and was profoundly effective. In the post-Christendom world it can still be effective, but has increasingly limited application. If the mission is accomplished, commissioning reverts to consolidation. Members are led deeper and deeper into the distant corners of the Bible, further and further into the nuances of Christian doctrine, wider and wider into the applications for public policy and ethical behavior. However, the post-Christendom church has discovered that the mission is not only still before us, but it has scarcely begun. There will be times and communities where membership consolidation is vitally important. The larger challenge today, as in ancient times, is mission and commission.

When the Common Lectionary is used for membership consolidation, alongside the cycles of the Uncommon Lectionary for mission outreach, the entire spectrum of worship options is enhanced. Experience has revealed, however, that when the Common Lectionary is used apart from a central focus on mission, then the value of membership consolidation is reduced to mere institutional survival. It is as if the Christendom world forgot what mission to the peoples immediately outside the doors of church looked like, and so its Common Lectionary worship lost the original theological context that made it vital. A Seeker Cycle and a Disciple Cycle became the forgotten pieces of a larger worship strategy. Once worship is restored to its original purpose as an act of mission, and these vital pieces are rediscovered, then the Common Lectionary once again becomes vital and valuable for the body of Christ.

A lectionary of any variety is more than just a plan for preaching. It is a mind-set. It is a time line in which all programs, curriculums, and leaders are deployed. It is a process around which congregational life is oriented. This is why it is so stressful to shift from the Common Lectionary to the Uncommon Lectionary. More is implied than just changing the Scriptures that will be the basis for the sermon. This is also why the breakdown in the use of the Common Lectionary leads to such confusion in the church. Preachers, worship designers, musicians, teachers, group leaders, and fellowship planners are suddenly working from conflicting agendas or diverging plans. What is needed is not only to align the whole church around a central plan, but also to make that plan not about membership assimilation but about mission outreach. A central plan that looks inward leads to decline. A central plan that looks outward leads to growth.

Great worship always leads to growth. Primarily, this is mission growth. It is the real impact of the church for personal and social change across the microcultures of the primary mission field. Yet this also implies numerical growth in membership and worship attendance, spiritual growth among members and leaders, and financial growth in programs and benevolences. Wherever you see this kind of holistic, dynamic growth, you always find great worship at the heart of the church. That worship may not always be as professional as people expect, or as dogmatically pure or politically correct as seminaries and denominations wish, but it is always authentic, dynamic, and part of a larger process of making disciples. Similarly, wherever you do *not* see this kind of holistic, dynamic growth, you will find merely good worship at the heart of the church. That worship may be highly professional, with superior quality, pure in doctrine, and correct in practice, and it might even be praised by seminaries and denominations—and yet the church is dying around it. Great worship happens when the church recognizes the spiritual hunger of the world, and commits itself to doing whatever it takes to help strangers to grace experience Christ.

Great worship is not a matter of style. Style has to do with the accoutrements of worship (music, clothing, hardware, hardwood, decorations, etc.). Great worship has to do with the intersection of the infinite and the finite, the experience of incarnation, and the discipline of the spiritual life. The plan for worship should encourage these three things. I have come to describe five signs of great worship, each one of which is supported by the cycles of the Uncommon Lectionary. Use these to measure the mission power of your worship strategy.

Great Worship Lets God Be God

How does one design an encounter with the uncontrollable Holy? Any structure is liable to be broken; any liturgy is liable to be interrupted; any form is liable to be shattered. God may seize anyone, any structure, and any process—use it, fill it, and discard it—for divine purposes that may be occasionally clear but are often mysterious. The great challenge to worship designers is to manage the event without overmanaging the event. The greatest mistake in worship design is to be surprised or annoyed by the unexpected. The greatest sin in worship design is to too hastily consider worship a success or failure based on the quality of our performance.

The Uncommon Lectionary, like any lectionary, anticipates that certain scriptures will be more revelatory of God's grace, at certain times of the year, than other scriptures. That is a presumption on the Holy, but an unavoidable one. It can at least be made with greater sensitivity to mission and greater flexibility for God's unexpected action. This is why the Uncommon Lectionary emphasizes the need to define your primary mission field and investigate the demographic and lifestyle diversity within it. Worship designers can choose scriptures that address the spiritual moments and flow of real life, rather than rely on scriptures chosen for a largely forgotten Christian year. Distant experts cannot do this. They cannot impose a calendar on a context. Ironically, a preaching schedule designed bottom up is more open to God's initiative top down. The more sensitive to the context you can be, the more open to God's creativity you can become.

> The challenge to professionally designed worship is that it becomes so good that it fails to be great.

Great Worship Brings Christ into Relationship

How does a human being form a relationship with God? Relationships are built around similarities, common interests, the possibility of serious conversation, and mutual recognition of the intrinsic worth that lies at the heart of two parties. To borrow a metaphor from Martin Luther, God having a relationship with humans is a little like humans having a relationship with worms. It's difficult to imagine. Humans and worms have nothing in common, and have no way to carry on a conversation. More important, worms do not appear to have an intrinsic self-worth that humans must respect. A valuable function, yes; a reason for self-esteem, no. The challenge in forming a relationship with God is that humans are more sinful than they think they are. This intrinsic *lack* of worth, and this profound reason for the *absence* of deserved self-esteem, is the original sin that undermines worship. It blocks an authentic relationship with God.

The Uncommon Lectionary, like any lectionary, is designed by radically sinful people (professional and amateur), for radically sinful people (clergy and lay). We are "worms" aspiring to be in relationship with God. The only way that will be possible is if God becomes human. Incarnation is the only way. Christ is the only way. We are never going to be in God, and God is never going to be in us, until we are altogether in Christ. Therefore, the Uncommon Lectionary is unapologetically Christocentric. Worship designers orient worship around an experience of Christ. Every worship service is designed with a metaphor for Christ. "Jesus' Purpose" is one of the five story lines of the Disciple Cycle, and the coming and return of Christ are the high points of salvation history. Why? Because Christ is the way to have a relationship with God.

The centrality of Christ in the Uncommon Lectionary does not preclude appreciation of other religions. Preachers can value their convictions and dialogue with their theologians. Christian worshipers can learn from their insights. Yet every religion has a framework within which it perceives life and interprets hope, and a key assumption or tenet of faith from which it dialogues with others. For Christians, that is Jesus Christ. Worship without Christ (i.e., without naming Jesus, modeling his behavior, and experiencing his real presence) is not Christian worship. It may be spiritual worship, and it may be profound worship, but it is not Christian worship. The specific rite of Eucharist may not be in every worship service to make it Christian, but Christ must be in every worship service to make it Christian.

> The challenge to institutionally designed worship is that when members pretend to be good, their worship fails to be great.

Great Worship Follows the Heart to the Mind

How do you know the truth, when truth is beyond human under-standing? Most modern worship is shaped entirely around words (spoken or written, recited or heard). Even when there are silences in modern worship, silence is defined by the *absence* of words. Silence is rarely "awesome." It is usually blessed relief from the steady barrage of words. There is a reason why worship is so wordy. Worship leaders are trying to be reasonable. Worshipers want their faith to be explain-able. After all, that is the standard of science in the age of rationality. To be sure, worship is often emotional. It can be cathartic or thera-peutic. Yet even then it is explainable as psychology. Words can still interpret the import of the rapid heartbeat, tearing eyes, and incom-prehensible outbursts.

The Uncommon Lectionary, like any lectionary, relies heavily on words to help disciples articulate and seekers under-stand their faith. Worship, after all, is a form of communication, and communi-cation must be intelligible. Nevertheless, truth is not something people really yearn to understand—it is something they yearn to *experience*. The Uncommon Lectionary assumes the data bank with which leaders resource great worship includes images, sounds, tastes, smells, and touchable objects. The primary learning methodology today is not lec-ture and reading, but conversation and

The challenge to modern worship is that really good preaching actually undermines the potential for worship to be great.

image. This lectionary does want to reach the mind and inform our understanding. It wants people to think, and to think hard, think cre-atively, and think profoundly. Yet the source of our reflection cannot be just words and abstractions, but pictures and metaphors and sen-sory experiences that equally illuminate truth. People today do not think to get motivated—they must be motivated to think.

Truth is ultimately a matter of the heart. The kind of knowledge seekers and disciples want is not an abstract theology or the catego-rization of Scriptures into socioeconomic, historical facts. They want to *know* in the ancient sense of that word. They want to merge, unite, or join with the internal constitution of God. They want human reason to interface with the depth of reason, the divine Logos that makes sense of life. They want to be grafted into the olive tree (Rom 11:24); be raised a glorious body (1 Cor 15:53); and walk the streets, smell the aromas, touch the flowers, and hear the joyous commotion of the New Jerusalem. The truth will provoke joy, but always escape mere words. This is poetry, and not prose, and certainly not preaching. Great worship causes Job to exclaim, "I know that my Redeemer lives, / and that at last he will stand upon the earth . . . then in my flesh I shall see God" (19:25-26).

Great Worship Gives Christians Courage

How do you inspire ordinary people to extraordinary virtue? Ancient people believed it couldn't be done. People were either born noble, or occasionally achieved virtue by incredible self-discipline. Even the church has always been ambivalent about sainthood. They refer to the "saints in worship," but don't really mean it. Saints are born or occasionally created, but they are certainly a different minority group from the ordinary members of the church. Saints are people who have a rare blood type, a unique Enneagram, or a peculiar Myers-Briggs personality type that makes them nicer, kinder, more forgiving, more tolerant, or more sacrificial than ordinary church members. Sometimes, as a reward for such model behavior, God will grant them miracles and the church will elect them to high office.

> Good worship inspires people to do good things, but great worship inspires people to become great leaders.

Yet sainthood is not about personality and sacrifice. It's about radical courage and persistence. This is what makes virtue attainable by ordinary folk. Saints simply have the courage to be Christian. Sometimes this is daring (being Christian in defiance of authority, or in support of victims, or raging against injustice), and sometimes this is habit (being Christian in the spontaneity of family life, or in the routine of work, or in leisure behavior). It is the ability to *endure* the persecution, indifference, jeering, mocking, or abuse—and *still* be

Christian. It is the ability to *repeat* unthinkingly, over and over again, patterns of behavior that are the fruits of the spirit of Christ.

This ambivalence about sainthood—and who is expected to model saintly behavior—is reflected in worship. Good worship is designed to motivate Christians to support the church, administer programs, and raise money so that the saints can do the ministries. Great worship is designed to motivate Christians to hear their own call to mission, model Christ in their daily living, and do the ministries themselves.

The Uncommon Lectionary, like any lectionary, is designed to build up the body of Christ. It is designed to motivate and equip the saints. Worship, however, is not a workshop to train skills or a classroom to teach ideas. It is the context to shape lifestyles, and the rally to grow leaders who can model lifestyles. This is why the Uncommon Lectionary focuses worship specifically on lifestyle, living daily life, daringly and spontaneously, counter to the culture that surrounds you. Worship inspires people to be daring, and encourages people to persist in an alternative, and sometimes highly criticized, habit of behavior. The requirement for small-group participation in the Disciple Cycle is intended to let leaders mentor disciples who will become mentors of other disciples and models for other seekers. "Who, me?" asks the ordinary church member. "Of course, you!" replies Christ. All that is required is courage—the courage to risk, dare, persist, and endure.

Great Worship Inspires Real Hope

How do you convince people to seriously believe in the impossible? Skepticism and cynicism permeate postmodern culture. All authorities are questioned, all assumptions are doubted, and all promises are temporary. The only certainties in life are death and taxes, and science is working on ways to delay the former, and lawyers are working on ways to circumvent the latter. This radical skepticism permeates Christian theology and mission today. It reveals that deep down inside Christian leaders at all levels of the church have put their trust in institutionalization (professional training and salary packages, property ownership and corporate protection, or progressive programming and charitable status), rather than in God's covenant.

As institutions crumble before the radical doubt of postmodern culture, institutional leaders grow ever more cynical about God's

> **The challenge to postmodern worship is that accommodation by church leaders to the cynicism of culture undermines their ability to lead great worship.**

promises for abundant life. Such cynicism permeates even Christian worship. It is not just that biblical scholars are analyzing Scripture into irrelevancy, or that church institutions have fractured into ridiculous ideological extremes. The discontinuity between the preacher's sermon and the preacher's life, and the discontinuity between the church member's liturgy during the service and the church member's attitude before and after service, is too great to deceive either the unchurched or the churched any longer. Christians don't really believe what they say, pray, preach, or proclaim.

The Uncommon Lectionary, like any lectionary, proclaims and interprets good news for the world. The question is whether that news is wishful thinking or real hope. Is it something that people wish might happen, but frankly do not expect any time soon, if ever? Or is it a serious expectation on which people are willing to stake their family security, personal careers, and very lives? This is why the Uncommon Lectionary requires worship designed to evolve *out of the spiritual life of a team*. It does not evolve out of quality training from the seminary or music college, or out of knowledge of church history, or out of a book approved by the denomination. It comes out of the spiritual life, leadership, and commitment of a team. The team may include a professional preacher or a professional musician, but it will also include unpaid volunteers who have nothing to gain by success except the assurance they are aligning their lives with God's will.

Great worship springs from the hearts, minds, and disciplined lives of spiritual leaders. These leaders demonstrate to the people that *they really believe this stuff!* They are prepared to stake their lives on it. God's covenant—this salvation history—that culminates in the incarnation of Jesus the Christ is reliable, trustworthy, and true. Their spiritual commitment is transparent and visible to the people in worship. The words and images, the stories and Scriptures, cannot be easily written off as wishful thinking or rejected as comforting old fantasies.

Somebody really means it. The seekers see that the disciples really mean it. The disciples see that their leaders really mean it. All the diversity of microcultures in the primary mission field see that the church really means it. Great worship depends on great leaders who are willing to stake everything to be with Jesus on the road to mission.

The Uncommon Lectionary is more than a discipline of Bible reading and preaching. It is a mind-set: the way churches think about spiritual life and mission. It is a plan: the way churches organize themselves for education, nurture, and outreach. Worship lies at the heart of what it means to be a church. The lectionary lies at the heart of what it means to worship. This one means that we are serious about spiritual growth, and earnest about outreach. We are commissioned to be in mission—and we are in mission in order to commission. The seekers will be transformed and grow to be disciples, and the disciples will go out to transform and draw seekers to Christ. It makes good worship great.

APPENDIX A

THE UNCOMMON LECTIONARY:

Seeker Cycle

Overall Strategy

1. Discover your primary mission field, as defined by the average distance or drive time people are willing to travel to work and shop.
2. Customize the spiritual calendar of the public, highlighting significant events for the various communities of the primary mission field.
3. Focus your heartburst for worship, for the microculture you earnestly desire to reach.
4. Focus your missional purpose—the experience of grace the target public yearns to have (e.g., healing, coaching, celebration, and so on).

Design of Worship

1. Feel absolutely free to customize for your context!
2. Focus Scriptures for the missional purpose of any given worship experience.

3. Concentrate on just one chunk of Scripture in any given worship experience.
4. Combine drama, music, and image with the spoken word.
5. Connect worship with follow-up small groups and spiritual disciplines.

Preparation of the Worship Design Team

1. Feel absolutely free to think, consult, and create!
2. Review the core values, beliefs, vision, and mission of the church.
3. Focus the meditation of the team in preparation for worship.
4. Mobilize additional teams to develop and deliver the message.
5. Immediately mingle with people following worship to coach and gain feedback.

Evaluation

• Has the worship helped strangers to grace experience God? Are people better off for the worship experience?
• Has the worship helped participants experience Jesus Christ?
• Has the worship helped participants understand, appreciate, or apply this basic text of the Bible to their daily lives?

The Uncommon Lectionary: Seeker Cycle

Spiritual Issues for worship themes are in normal lettering; Spiritual Issues for leadership teams are in italics.

Week	Worship Theme	Target Public	Worship Team Meditation	Missional Purpose	Spiritual Issue	Public Calendar
(January) 1	Genesis 1–2		Acts 17		New beginnings; *Discerning the unknown*	New Year's
2	Colossians 1:15–2:19		Luke 2:21-38		Your experience with Jesus; *The point of it all*	Empty Nester Holidays
3	John 8:12-20; 9		Luke 10:1-24		Hope for the future; *Risking all for the gospel*	
4	Jeremiah 18:1-11		Luke 9:57-62		God shapes our lives; *Being a disciple*	Super Bowl
5	Acts 9:1-31		Luke 12:1-12		God can totally change us; *Trusting spontaneity*	
(February) 6	Romans 1:16, 17; 8:1-39		Luke 4:1-15		Total commitment; *Resisting secret selfishness*	Chinese New Year

Week	Worship Theme	Target Public	Worship Team Meditation	Missional Purpose	Spiritual Issue	Public Calendar
7	Deuteronomy 5:1-21; 6:1-9		Luke 12:35–13:5		The basic rules; *Leadership credibility*	Ground Hog Day
8	Luke 15:11-32		Luke 19:1-10		Grace beyond rules; *Leadership humility*	Valentine's Day
9	Hosea 4; 14		Luke 7:36-50		Ultimate acceptance; *Everyone has a ministry*	Oscar Night
(March) 10	Romans 12		Acts 27; 28:1-16		Why Christ is crucial; *Leadership courage*	School Break
11	Isaiah 52–53		Luke 21:7-19; 22:1-6		Servant leadership; *Leadership vindication*	St. Patrick's Day
12	Matthew 16:24–17:23		Luke 18:31-43; 19:28-44		What a "Savior" is; *Take up the cross*	Passover
13	Luke 24:36-53; Acts 1:1-11		Mark 14		The "Jesus" story; *Step out in confidence*	Easter
(April) 14	John 19–20		Luke 22:7-23		Significance of the story; *Extreme communion*	April Fool's Day

Week	Worship Theme	Target Public	Worship Team Meditation	Missional Purpose	Spiritual Issue	Public Calendar
15	Luke 24:1-35		Acts 13–14		Where Jesus went; *Spiritually yearning public*	Income Tax USA
16	Ezekiel 34		Luke 15:1-7		God's inclusive love; *God's specific love*	Sports Play-offs
17	1 Corinthians 15		Luke 20:27-40		Our hope for eternal life; *Life after death*	Ballpark Openings
18	Isaiah 55		Acts 8:4-40		Real living starts now; *The meaning of baptism*	Earth Day, Income Tax Canada
(May) 19	Mark 10:1-31; John 8:1-11		Luke 8:19-21		The Christian family; *Divine relationships*	May Day
20	Proverbs 3		Luke 17:11-19		Where good advice comes from; *Real gratitude*	Mother's Day
21	Genesis 17:1–18:15		Luke 13:22-30		Roots of true community; *Tough choices*	Victoria Day
22	Acts 2; 3; 4:32-37		Acts 10; 11; 15		Hope of true community; *Outreach to pagan world*	Memorial Day

Week	Worship Theme	Target Public	Worship Team Meditation	Missional Purpose	Spiritual Issue	Public Calendar
(June) 23	1 Corinthians 12; 13; 14		Luke 21:1-4		Who you really are; *What you really give*	
24	Micah 6		Luke 10:25-37		Where duty really lies; *Your fundamental obligation*	Father's Day
25	1 Peter 2; 5		Luke 13:31-55; 18:9-14		Being truly blessed; *Real life choices*	St. Jean Baptiste Day
26	Matthew 28:16-20		Acts 18:24—19:41		What God expects; *Measuring results*	
(July) 27	Isaiah 6		Acts 23:12—26:32		Seeing your call; *Perseverance*	Canada Day
28	James 1—2		Luke 20:9-26		Real integrity; *God's method of reward*	Independence Day
29	1 Samuel 16—17		Luke 20:41-47		Living up to standards; *Overcoming pride*	
30	John 4:1-42		Acts 3:1—4:31		Why Jesus matters; *God's healing power*	Local Fairs
31	Habakkuk 2:1-5; 3		Acts 18		Looking to the future; *Assessing your team*	

Week	Worship Theme	Target Public	Worship Team Meditation	Missional Purpose	Spiritual Issue	Public Calendar
(August) 32	John 14:1–15:17		Luke 13:18-19; 17:5-6		Relationship to Christ; *Anticipating results*	Local Fairs
33	Job 1; 2; 3; 40; 41; 42		Luke 16:19-31		Coping with evil; *Setting priorities*	
34	Philippians 2:1-18; 3		Acts 16		Life worth living; *Postmodern paradigm*	
35	2 Corinthians 4–5		Luke 18:18-30		Wealth in perspective; *Staking your safety net*	Back to School
(September) 36	Exodus 1; 2; 3		Luke 5:27-32; 6:12-16; 8:1-3, 19-21		Discerning your destiny; *Right person at right time*	Labor Day
37	Matthew 5; 6; 7		Luke 6		Gospel in a nutshell; *Jesus' basic message*	9/11 Remembrance
38	Ezekiel 37:1-14		Luke 8:4-15, 22-56		What God wants to do; *Jesus is Lord over conflict*	Rosh Hashanah
39	Luke 9:10-17		Luke 14:15-24		Strangers welcome here; *Who gets honored most*	

Week	Worship Theme	Target Public	Worship Team Meditation	Missional Purpose	Spiritual Issue	Public Calendar
(October)						
40	Ecclesiastes 3		Luke 12:22-34		God is in control; *Stress reduction*	Thanksgiving (CN)
41	Revelation 21:1—22:7		Luke 17:20-37		What happens when he returns; Look for the Kingdom now	Yom Kippur
42	Amos 5		Luke 14:1-14, 25-35		Radical justice; *Imitating Jesus*	Harvest Fairs
43	Galatians 5:1—6:10		Luke 6:27-49		Real life morality; *Extreme love*	
44	1 Kings 17; 18; 19		Luke 7:18-35		What prophets really do; *Pointing to Jesus*	Ramadan
(November)						
45	John 11:1—12:11		Acts 20:7-12		How the dead are raised; *Attending to little things*	Halloween
46	2 Kings 4—5		Luke 4:31—5:26		Supernatural experiences; *Fishing for microcultures*	Remembrance Day
47	1 John 3:11—5:5		Luke 11:14-36		All-powerful love; *Mission consistency*	Thanksgiving Day (US)
48	Isaiah 9:1-7; 11:1-9		Luke 21:25-36		Why Christmas matters; *Be alert*	

Week	Worship Theme	Target Public	Worship Team Meditation	Missional Purpose	Spiritual Issue	Public Calendar
(December) 49	Luke 1		Acts 28:17-31		The First Christmas carols; *Laying it on the line*	World AIDS Day
50	John 1		Luke 22:39-46; 23:26-49		Fully divine, fully human; *Fully human, fully divine*	Christmas Parties
51	Luke 2:1-20		Acts 14		How Jesus came; *Leaders are NOT divine*	Hanukkah
52	Matthew 1:18–2:23		Luke 9:18-36		Adoring Christ; *Magical moments*	Christmas Eve

APPENDIX B

THE UNCOMMON LECTIONARY:

Disciple Cycle

Overall Strategy

1. Weeks are numbered 1 to 52. Designated months may vary as some months have five Sundays. Keep following the numbered weeks.
2. The cycle starts with week 19 at the beginning of the first story line, and follows a calendar most relevant to the pace of contemporary culture.
3. There are five major story lines for worship teaching and small-group discussion. Review all the texts for small-group exploration.
4. Orient worship to coach faith, hope, or lifestyle as the Spirit leads. Try to diversify the focus through the year. Add to the primary text as called.
5. Ground worship in the experience of Jesus as the Spirit leads. Try to diversify the focus through the year.

Design of Worship

1. Build on the basic text using sources from the small-group study.
2. Focus the worship around faith, hope, or lifestyle.
3. Combine drama, music, and image with the spoken word.
4. Link with small-group discussion.

Preparation of the Worship Design Team

1. Feel absolutely free to think, consult, and create!
2. Review the core values, beliefs, vision, and mission of the church.
3. Ground the worship in the experience of Christ.
4. Link with training small-group leaders.

Preparation for Small Groups

1. Read all the texts ahead of time.
2. Set the texts in the overall context of the story line.
3. Select specific parts of the story or specific texts for focus this year, depending on faith, hope, or lifestyle coaching and the key experience of Christ in worship.

Evaluation

- Has the worship effectively communicated faith, or inspired hope, or shaped lifestyle for the participants?
- Has the worship helped participants experience Jesus Christ?
- Has the worship informed and enhanced small-group discussion during the week?

The Uncommon Lectionary: Disciple Cycle

Weekly story lines are in normal lettering;
Five major story lines are underlined.

Week	Worship Theme	Faith, Hope, Lifestyle	Worship Team Meditation	Way of Christ	Small-Group Study	Story Line
						<u>Israel's Covenant</u>
(May) 19	Genesis 1:1-31		1 Corinthians 15:20-25, 35-49		Genesis 1–3; 7–8	Creation to Noah
20	Genesis 17:1-21		John 8:39-58		Genesis 15; 17:1–18:15; 21:1-7; 22:1-19	Covenant of Abram; Isaac's Sacrifice
21	Genesis 28:10-22; 32:22-32; 33:1-11		Hebrews 11:1, 8-39; 12:1-14		Genesis 25:19-34; 27; 28:10-22; 32:3–33:16	Jacob's Story
22	Genesis 45:1-28		Mark 3:7-19, 31-35		Genesis 37; 39–50	Joseph's Story
(June) 23	Exodus 3:1-17		Luke 9:28-50		Exodus 1:1–4:17	Moses' Call
24	Exodus 12:1-39		Matthew 14:1-33		Exodus 4:18–6:13; 6:28–14:31	Passover and Exodus
25	Numbers 20:1-13		John 4:7-42		Numbers 11:1–14:25; 17; 20; 22; 27:12-23	Water from the rock, Balaam's Oracle
26	Deuteronomy 10:12-22; 11:18-21		Romans 7:4-25		Exodus 15; 20; 32; 34; Deuteronomy 10:10–11:32	God's Commandments

Week	Worship Theme	Faith, Hope, Lifestyle	Worship Team Meditation	Way of Christ	Small-Group Study	Story Line
(July) 27	Joshua 24:1-32		Luke 6:27-49		Joshua 1:20; 23; 24; Judges 5–8; 14–16	Conquest, Recovenant, Judges
						David's Legacy
28	Ruth 1:1-17; 4:13-17		John 13:1-20, 31-35		Ruth	David's heritage
29	1 Samuel 1:19-27; 3:1-21		Acts 22:3-21; 26:2-18		1 Samuel 1–3	Call of Samuel
30	1 Samuel 10:14-24		1 Peter 2:1-10		1 Samuel 8–10; 15:10-35	Saul
31	1 Samuel 16:1–17:58		2 Timothy 2:1-15		1 Samuel 16–21; 31	David's struggle with Saul
(August) 32	2 Samuel 7:1-29		1 Timothy 1:12-17; 3:10-13; 6:11-16		2 Samuel 5–7; 11–12; 18	King David
33	Psalms 22; 23		1 Thessalonians 5:1-24		1 Kings 1:1–3:28; 8; Psalms 1; 8; 19; 22; 23; 42; 46; 77	Solomon and the Temple
34	1 Kings 19:1-21		2 Corinthians 11:21–12:10		1 Kings 16:29–22:40	Elijah and Ahab
35	2 Kings 5:1-14		Luke 4:23-30; 17:12-19		2 Kings 2; 4:1–5:19; 13:14-21	Elisha and Naaman

Week	Worship Theme	Faith, Hope, Lifestyle	Worship Team Meditation	Way of Christ	Small-Group Study	Story Line
(September)						
36	2 Kings 19:20-34; Psalm 137		John 15:1-27		2 Kings 17; 18–20; 25; Psalm 137; 2 Chronicles 36:15-23	Fall of Israel and Judah
37	Psalms 91; 139		2 Corinthians 4:1-18		Psalms 84; 91; 96; 100; 116; 121; 139	Hope and faithfulness
						Faithful Servants
38	Amos 5:18-24; 7:7-9		Matthew 10:1-42		Amos 1; 5; 7	Justice and God's Plumb Line
39	Hosea 11; 14		Luke 17:1-6; 18:9-17		Hosea 1; 4; 6; 8; 14	Sin and returning to the Lord
(October)						
40	Micah 5:1-4; 6:1-8		Ephesians 4:1–5:1-2		Micah 1; 4–7	What the Lord requires
41	Job 19; 42:1-6		1 Corinthians 15:42-58		Job 1–2; 13–14; 19; 38; 40–42	The problem of evil and suffering
42	Nehemiah 8:1-12		1 Corinthians 1:18-31; 2:1-16; 3:1-23		Ezra; Nehemiah 8; Ecclesiastes 3; Proverbs 8–15	Return of the exiles and true wisdom
43	Jeremiah 31:27-34		Luke 14:15-35		Jeremiah 11–13; 17:5-18; 18:1-6; 31:27-34	The Potter's Clay and calls to repentance
44	Isaiah 6:1-8		John 6:41-69		Isaiah 1; 6:1-8; 9; 11	God's call and promises

Week	Worship Theme	Faith, Hope, Lifestyle	Worship Team Meditation	Way of Christ	Small-Group Study	Story Line
(November)						
45	Isaiah 41:1-13		Philippians 4:4-13		Isaiah 30:1-18; 35 40–42; 45	God's assurance of love and redemption
46	Isaiah 55:1-13		Romans 10:1-17		Isaiah 52–53; 55; 58:1-9; 61:1-11	God's grace and forgiveness
						Jesus' Purpose
47	Colossians 1:1-23		Isaiah 25:1-9; 26:1-3		Luke 1; Colossians 1:13-23	Jesus Messiah and Christ
48	John 19:16-30; 20:11-18		Isaiah 53:1-12		John 18–20; Matthew 27:1-54; Hebrews 8	The Significance of Jesus' death
(December)						
49	Luke 4:16-30		Isaiah 42:1-9; Psalm 22		Luke 4:16-43; Matthew 5–7; Galatians 5	Jesus preaching and modeling
50	John 8:12; 9:1-41		Isaiah 60:1-5, 19-22		John 8–10; 1 John 1:5–2:17	Light of the World
51	1 Corinthians 13		Hosea 11:1-4; 8-12		John 14–16; 1 Corinthians 11–14	The love of Jesus
52	Luke 2:1-20		Isaiah 9:1-7		Matthew 1:18–2:23; Luke 1–2; Philippians 3:1–4:7	The birth of Jesus

Week	Worship Theme	Faith, Hope, Lifestyle	Worship Team Meditation	Way of Christ	Small-Group Study	Story Line
(January)						
1	Luke 13:22-30; 15:11-32		Habakkuk 2:1-4; 3:17-19		Luke 13–15; 18; Romans 12	The hope of Jesus
2	1 Peter 2:1-10		Psalm 27		John 2–5; 1 Peter 1; 1 John 4	The inner meaning of Jesus
3	Mark 4:1-9, 26-41		Ezekiel 34:1-31		Mark 1–5; Ephesians 2	The acts of Jesus
4	Mark 6:30-52		Deuteronomy 10:10–11:7		Mark 6–9; James 1	The teachings of Jesus
5	Mark 10:13-34		Isaiah 11:1-9		Mark 10–13; Romans 8	The significance of Jesus
(February)						
6	John 1		Zechariah 9:9-10		John 1; 1 Corinthians 3	The Lordship of Jesus
						Christians' Mission
7	Acts 1:6-11; Matthew 28:16-20		2 Kings 2:1-12		Matthew 28; Luke 24; Acts 1; 1 Peter; 1 John	Great Commission
8	Acts 2:1-13, 37-47		Joel 2:28-29		Luke 14; Acts 2:1–6:7; James; Romans 12–15	First growth of the church
9	Galatians 5:1-25		Isaiah 49:8-13		Acts 8–12; Galatians	Emergence of apostles and outreach

Week	Worship Theme	Faith, Hope, Lifestyle	Worship Team Meditation	Way of Christ	Small-Group Study	Story Line
(March)						
10	2 Corinthians 4:1–6:13		Jonah		Acts 13:1–15:35; 2 Corinthians	Missionaries in a pagan world
11	Acts 16		Micah 4:1-7		Acts 15:36–16:40; Philippians	Paradigm of church growth
12	John 13:1-35		Isaiah 55:1-13		Acts 17–18; Matthew 25; 27; John 6; 13	Eucharist and Gentile mission
13	Ephesians 2:1-22; 6:10-20		Ezekiel 36:37–37:28		Acts 19–20; John 20; 1 Corinthians; Ephesians	Resurrection and explaining salvation
(April)						
14	2 Timothy 1:1–2:13; 4:1-5		Proverbs 2:1-22		Acts 21–26; John 21; 1 and 2 Timothy	Leadership in mission
15	Colossians 3:1-17		Psalm 121		Acts 27–28; Colossians 1–4	Victory and new life in Christ
16	Romans 1:16-17; 5:1-11		Psalms 42; 56		Romans 1–5; Revelation 1–3	Righteousness by faith
17	Romans 8:1-39		Psalm 51		Romans 7–8; John 11–12; Deuteronomy 5:1–6:9	Law and Grace
18	1 Thessalonians 4:1–5:24		Jeremiah 31:7-14; 33:14-16		Romans 10–11; 1 Thessalonians; Revelation 21–22	Eternal hope and the end of time

APPENDIX C

Adapting the Uncommon Lectionary to the Southern Hemisphere

The exercise of adapting the Uncommon Lectionary cycles to the Australian year is helpful to church leaders in a cultural context that is even more alienated from Christendom than Canada and the United States. However, it is also a useful teaching exercise to demonstrate how church leaders must be creative to adapt the lectionary to whatever context of mission God has entrusted to them. In a sense, the blessing of the Uncommon Lectionary, in contrast to the Common Lectionary, is precisely its nontransferability. It cannot simply be borrowed from one culture and applied to another. It must be customized.

Therefore, the Uncommon Lectionary cycles are much more demanding of the spiritual life and cultural sensitivity of congregational leaders. It is no longer possible to simply ignore pop culture and focus on feast days. Nor is it possible to skip over intense religious dialogue with culture and concentrate on dogmatic theology. All worship planning starts with a very simple, practical question: "Who is Jesus, and why should he matter to my microculture?"

The challenge to adapting the two cycles of the Uncommon Lectionary to Australia is not simply that seasons are reversed. Both multiculturalism and regionalism are more advanced than in North America (even more advanced than in Canada) and the English-speaking culture includes, distorts, and adds to the British heritage in unexpected ways. Waves of migration have shaped the Australian continent more dramatically, and in a shorter span of time, than in North America. When one considers the origins of the first settlements and convict colonies; and then the growth of succeeding settlements through the immigration of desperate peoples seeking new life; and then the growth of modern cities influenced by the expansion of overflowing southeast Asian cultures; and all this happening in a relatively short span of time; one feels the contrast with North America. In North America, culture was shaped by European wars, religious motivations, and desire for a better life. In Australia, culture was shaped by exploration, legal systems, and a desire to survive. One has the sense that the heart of Australia is at once more passionate and more reasonable than the heart of North America. Immigrants to Canada and the United States were motivated by pragmatism and ended up being consumers. Immigrants to Australia either really, really didn't want to be there and had no choice; or they really, really wanted to be there and chose this destination *over* easier options for Canada and the United States. They were motivated by adventure and ended up being synthesizers of many cultures. It is no accident that new American products are often test-marketed in Australia first, where they are refined and focused for export back to the Northern Hemisphere.

In my view, the church generally has ignored the actual flow of the calendar year and annual life experience, and imposed an artificial cycle of planning, development, and evaluation for its programs that is out of step with culture. The more alienated culture becomes from the church, the more difficult it becomes for church leaders to effectively grow congregational mission.

Both in North America and Australia, churches assumed that planning and development would happen in February and March when, supposedly, agricultural work was at low ebb and people had nothing better to do than Lenten disciplines. They would implement and develop programs through the ensuing months, celebrate feast days to coincide with the harvest (supposedly in the fall), and evaluate the results in January. At that time they would form a new budget and start all over again.

We already know that these assumptions do not work in North America. People tend to be on holiday from June through August, and plans initiated in April or May are soon forgotten. Planning really begins in September; implementation and development extend through the next seven months. Evaluation in January is premature, but the church fails to do it in April and May.

In Australia, the situation is different yet again. Visioning and mission discernment begins in June (not February), and ends in September when North American leaders are just getting started. Strategic planning for these initiatives unfolds from October through January. This is the time when Australia is preparing for, or already enjoying, summer. In North America, these months are times of frantic activity and program implementation, but in Australia these months are times to pause; reflect; reconsider core values, beliefs, vision, and mission; work through anxieties about transitioning from old habits to new tactics; research and understand demographic trends; and nurture members or refresh leaders of the church.

Implementation and program development accelerates from February through May. This is the time of highest enthusiasm and energy for continuing education. People are starting new jobs, relocating to new places, and beginning academic courses. Curriculums are launched, and mission experiments are tested. By June the results will begin to be evaluated, and as the programs continue to adjust and focus, leaders will begin to re-vision the coming cycle of mission. The end of the financial year, and income tax deadlines, occur in June, setting the stage for leaders to develop the next budget.

The contrast in the annual cycle of life has changed over time, and from place to place. The classic patterns might look something like this:

	Old Christendom	North America	Australia
Visioning	Jan.-March (Lent)	Sept.-Nov. (Thanksgiving)	June-Sept. (Football Finals)
Development	April-June (Pentecost)	Jan.-April (Mothers Day)	Oct.-Jan. (Australia Day)
Implementation	July-Nov. (Christ/King)	May-Aug. (Leisure Time)	Feb.-May (Anzac Day)

I am quite sure that readers from both North America and Australia will object that this is not *really* the cycle that is lived out today in their local contexts. In part, this is because every local and regional context is increasingly distinct, and the common national patterns are simply breaking down. However, it is also true that the encroachment of the "pagan" or "non-Christian spiritual world" is accelerating rapidly in all contexts.

This is more visible when one notes the emerging dominant holidays (i.e., "holy days" in the experience of popular culture). In the old Christendom world that lasted until World War I, the holy days were clearly Christian, and vacations were measured in hours and days. In North American experience (Canada and United States), the "holy days" are grounded in civil religion with a mixture of Christianity, nationalism, and nostalgia for childhood memories. In Australia, the "holy days" have drifted even further from Christian sensibilities and are grounded in sports and national, regional, or tribal pride. In both North America and Australia, vacations are now measured in weeks and months. The old Christendom world assumed that people took a vacation in order to *enjoy* their religion. Today in North America and Australia people take a vacation in order to *escape* their religion.

The result is that even the above calendar no longer corresponds to what is happening in culture. Major pieces of the mission planning and implementation cycle go missing.

- North Americans do visioning and program development very well, but the implementation phase coincides with summer vacation. Implementation is delayed to overlap with the time once devoted to visioning and strategic development of programs. This increases stress and conflict in the church. New strategic plans are being invented at the same time that old strategic plans are still being implemented and evaluated. In my view, American churches are like butterflies flitting from one great idea to the next, but never working long enough to follow through on any plan.

- Australians do strategic planning and implementation very well, but the visioning phase gets lost in the rush of public and private life, sports and self-interest. Visioning is delayed to overlap with time once devoted for strategic development and implementation. This reduces the clarity and consensus about values and beliefs that is a foundation of trust, and polarizes leaders who are traditionalists and mavericks. In my view, Australian churches are like koalas—methodically stripping the leaves from tree after tree, but unclear what their future role might be in the changing cultural forest.

One might speculate about the Canadian church experience in this evolving calendar. In my view, Canadian churches combine the worst and best of both worlds. On the one hand, Canadian churches have reduced both visioning and implementation into a continuous strategic dialogue that is unclear about christological assumptions and uncertain about missiological goals. The established church loses both its visionaries and entrepreneurs, but multiplies its bureaucrats. On the other hand, Canadian churches have combined American church innovation and Australian church tenacity that anticipates a new form of Christian community around faith-based nonprofit organizations.

The Seeker Cycle

The annual cycle of personal and public life in Australia is nuanced in at least five important ways to make the calendar different from North American experience. Like Canada, Australia is certainly more diverse than the United States with strong regional identities. Like North America in general, the competition for the spiritual interest of the public is significant, with new religious groups emerging, traditional established religions of all kinds growing, and Christianity receding from dominant influence. In that context, the following nuances are important:

1. *Sport.* Participation and enthusiasm for sports has replaced religion as a primary vehicle for friendship, purpose, and identity. It is a major affinity for small and large group gatherings that stirs emotion as nothing else can. It is not difficult to understand sport as a larger symbol of life struggle and personal hope, and of group pride and personal self-esteem. Australian rules football dominates the media year-round, and major events like the Melbourne Cup give permission to otherwise conservative people to behave extravagantly.

2. *Global and multicultural awareness.* Australians observe global and multicultural celebrations with greater enthusiasm than North Americans. Australian culture is extremely conscious of the diversity of Southeast Asia as partners in trade and politics. Like Canada, Australians are much more sensitive to aboriginal issues and religious observances.

3. *Recreation, environment, and family life.* Crosscultural influences in Australian culture are generally united in supporting strong family relationships that are traditional in terms of respect for elders; cooperative equality between parents; moral commitments that place the family unit above individual desires. The Australian family is more likely to share leisure time together, away from technology and in the midst of nature, with a keen sense of responsibility for the environment.

4. *Dramatic seasonal change.* Australian seasonal change tends to happen quickly and dramatically. The April/May and October/November transitions sharply contrast "wet and dry" or "green and brown," with subsequent impact on the emotions and attitudes of people. Seasonal change in North America is generally more gradual and less extreme. It is something to be enjoyed and managed. Seasonal change in Australia is more sudden and sensational. It is something to be experienced and endured.

5. *The paradox of the "center."* Australians are generally more open, receptive, and welcoming to other cultures beyond their borders. North Americans regard the beach as the boundary of their lives,

but most of the population of Australia lives close to the sea and readily connects with cultures beyond its shores. It is the interior that is the real boundary and the outback that is the unknown. The edge of adventure is really at the center of the continent. Americans and Canadians find themselves by going beyond their shores; Australians find themselves by journeying inland to Uluru (Ayers Rock).

I have little doubt that my observations will seem simplistic to Australian church leaders—just as their observations of Canadian and American culture may seem like overgeneralizations for people in North America. My point is not to provide a definitive interpretation of Australian culture, but rather to demonstrate the kind of thinking church leaders must undertake to adapt the Uncommon Lectionary cycles to their context. It is particularly important to connect the Seeker Cycle with the rhythms and meanings of public and personal life.

The Uncommon Lectionary: Seeker Cycle

Overall Strategy

1. Discover your primary mission field, as defined by the average distance or drive time people are willing to travel to work and shop.
2. Customize the spiritual calendar of the public, highlighting significant events for the various communities of the primary mission field.
3. Focus your heartburst for worship, for the microculture you earnestly desire to reach.
4. Focus your missional purpose—the experience of grace the target public yearns to have (e.g., healing, coaching, celebration, and so on).

Design of Worship

1. Feel absolutely free to customize for your context!
2. Focus scriptures for the missional purpose of any given worship experience.

3. Concentrate on just one chunk of Scripture in any given worship experience.
4. Combine drama, music, and image with the spoken word.
5. Connect worship with follow-up small groups and spiritual disciplines.

Preparation of the Worship Design Team

1. Feel absolutely free to think, consult, and create!
2. Review the core values, beliefs, vision, and mission of the church.
3. Focus the meditation of the team in preparation for worship.
4. Mobilize additional teams to develop and deliver the message.
5. Immediately mingle with people following worship to coach and gain feedback.

Evaluation

- Has the worship helped strangers to grace experience God? Are people better off for the worship experience?
- Has the worship helped participants experience Jesus Christ?
- Has the worship helped participants understand, appreciate, or apply this basic text of the Bible to their daily life?

The Uncommon Lectionary: Seeker Cycle for Australia

Spiritual Issues for worship themes are in normal lettering; Spiritual Issues for leadership teams are in italics.

Week	Worship Theme	Target Public	Worship Team Meditation	Missional Purpose	Spiritual Issue	Public Calendar
(January) 1	Matthew 5; 6; 7		Luke 6		Gospel in a nutshell; *Jesus' basic message*	Holiday Festivities
2	Ezekiel 37:1-14		Luke 8:4-15, 22-56		What God wants to do; *Jesus is Lord over conflict*	National Awards and Honors
3	Luke 9:10-17		Luke 14:15-24		Strangers welcome here; *Who gets honored most*	
4	Ecclesiastes 3		Luke 12:22-34		God is in control; *Stress reduction*	Australia Day
5	Revelation 21:1– 22:7		Luke 17:20-37		What happens when he returns; *Look for the Kingdom now*	Summer Holiday Ends
(February) 6	Genesis 1–2		Acts 17		New beginnings: *Discerning the unknown*	School Year Starts
7	Colossians 1:15– 2:19		Luke 2:21-38		Your experience with Jesus; *The point of it all*	Waitangi Day (NZ) Chinese New Year

Week	Worship Theme	Target Public	Worship Team Meditation	Missional Purpose	Spiritual Issue	Public Calendar
8	John 8:12-20; 9		Luke 10:1-24		Hope for the future; *Risking all for the gospel*	Valentine's Day
9	Jeremiah 18:1-11		Luke 9:57-62		God shapes our lives; *Being a disciple*	
(March) 10	Acts 9:1-31		Luke 12:1-12		God can totally change us; *Trusting spontaneity*	Change of Season Arts Festival
11	Romans 1:16, 17; 8:1-39		Luke 4:1-15		Total commitment; *Resisting secret selfishness*	Ethnic Cultural Group Festivals
12	Matthew 16:24—17:23		Luke 18:31-43; 19:28-44		What a Savior is; *Take up the cross*	Gay & Lesbian Mardi Gras (Sydney)
13	Luke 24:36-53; Acts 1:1-11		Mark 14		The Jesus story; *Step out in confidence*	Football Season Begins
(April) 14	John 19—20		Luke 22:7-23		Significance of the story; *Extreme communion*	April Fool's Day
15	Luke 24:1-35		Acts 13—14		Where Jesus went; *Spiritually yearning public*	Easter

Week	Worship Theme	Target Public	Worship Team Meditation	Missional Purpose	Spiritual Issue	Public Calendar
16	Ezekiel 34		Luke 15:1-7		God's inclusive love; *God's specific love*	Anzac Day
17	1 Corinthians 15		Luke 20:27-40		Our hope for eternal life; *Life after death*	Earth Day
18	Isaiah 55		Acts 8:4-40		Real living starts now; *The meaning of baptism*	
(May) 19	Mark 10:1-31; John 8:1-11		Luke 8:19-21		The Christian family; *Divine relationships*	Mother's Day
20	Proverbs 3		Luke 17:11-19		Where good advice comes; *Real gratitude*	Agricultural Fairs (NE Australia)
21	Genesis 17:1– 18:15		Luke 13:22-30		Roots of true community; *Tough choices*	
22	Acts 2; 3; 4:32-37		Acts 10; 11; 15		Hope of true community; *Outreach to pagan world*	
(June) 23	1 Corinthians 12; 13; 14		Luke 21:1-4		Who you really are; *What you really give*	Queen's Birthday
24	Micah 6		Luke 10:25-37		Where duty really lies; Your fundamental obligation	

Week	Worship Theme	Target Public	Worship Team Meditation	Missional Purpose	Spiritual Issue	Public Calendar
25	1 Peter 2; 5		Luke 13:31-55; 18:9-14		Being truly blessed; *Real life choices*	Income Tax Returns Due
26	Matthew 28:16-20		Acts 18:24–19:41		What God expects; *Measuring results*	
(July) 27	Isaiah 6		Acts 23:12–26:32		Seeing your call; *Perseverance*	
28	Deuteronomy 5:1-21; 6:1-9		Luke 12:35–13:5		The basic rules: *Leadership credibility*	
29	Luke 15:11-32		Luke 19:1-10		Grace beyond rules; *Leadership humility*	
30	Hosea 4; 14		Luke 7:36-50		Ultimate acceptance; *Everyone has a ministry*	
31	Romans 12		Acts 27; 28:1-16		Why Christ is crucial; *Leadership courage*	
(August) 32	Isaiah 52–53		Luke 21:7-19; 22:1-6		Servant leadership; *Leadership vindication*	
33	James 1–2		Luke 20:9-26		Real integrity; *God's method of reward*	

Week	Worship Theme	Target Public	Worship Team Meditation	Missional Purpose	Spiritual Issue	Public Calendar
34	1 Samuel 16–17		Luke 20:41-47		Living up to standards; *Over-coming pride*	
35	John 4:1-42		Acts 3:1–4:31		Why Jesus matters; *God's healing power*	
(September) 36	Habakkuk 2:1-5; 3		Acts 18		Looking to the future; *Assessing your team*	Father's Day
37	John 14:1–15:17		Luke 13:18-19; 17:5-6		Relationship to Christ; *Anticipating results*	Football Finals
38	Job 1; 2; 3; 40; 41; 42		Luke 16:19-31		Coping with evil; Setting priorities	Agricultural Fairs (Southern Australia)
39	Philippians 2:1-18; 3		Acts 16		Life worth living; *Post-modern paradigm*	Grand Final
(October) 40	2 Corinthians 4–5		Luke 18:18-30		Wealth in perspective; *Staking your safety net*	Eight Hours Day (Labor Day)
41	Exodus 1; 2; 3		Luke 5:27-32; 6:12-16; 8:1-3; 19-21		Discerning your destiny; *Right person at right time*	

Week	Worship Theme	Target Public	Worship Team Meditation	Missional Purpose	Spiritual Issue	Public Calendar
42	John 11:1–12:11		Acts 20:7-12		How the dead are raised; *Attending to little things*	
43	2 Kings 4–5		Luke 4:31–5:26		Supernatural experiences; *Fishing for microcultures*	
44	1 John 3:11–5:5		Luke 11:14-36		All-powerful love; *Mission consistency*	
(November) 45	Amos 5		Luke 14:1-14, 25-35		Radical Justice; *Imitating Jesus*	Melbourne Cup
46	Galatians 5:1–6:10		Luke 6:27-49		Real life morality; *Extreme love*	Schoolies Week (School break)
47	1 Kings 17; 18; 19		Luke 7:18-35		What prophets really do; *Pointing to Jesus*	Change of Season
48	Isaiah 9:1-7; 11:1-9		Luke 21:25-36		Why Christmas matters; *Be alert*	
(December) 49	Luke 1		Acts 28:17-31		The first Christmas carols; *Laying it on the line*	World AIDS Day Christmas Parties
50	John 1		Luke 22:39-46; 23:26-49		Fully divine, fully human; *Fully human, fully divine*	Hanukkah

Week	Worship Theme	Target Public	Worship Team Meditation	Missional Purpose	Spiritual Issue	Public Calendar
51	Luke 2:1-20		Acts 14		How Jesus came; *Leaders are NOT divine*	Christmas Eve
52	Matthew 1:18–2:23		Luke 9:18-36		Adoring Christ; *Magical moments*	Summer Holidays begin

The Disciple Cycle

It should be obvious that the Disciple Cycle places the study of "Jesus' Purpose" and "Christians' Mission" at precisely the months usually associated with visioning and strategic development of programs. These are the months in the year in which there is the greatest energy for disciplined learning and leadership development, new initiatives, and program development.

In North America, these months will be November through April. Christmas is at the heart of this period. North Americans tend to look to Christmas (not Easter) as the revelatory moment for the person and work of Christ, and as the motivational moment that will inspire the study and mission outreach for the rest of the year. The old Christendom world assumed that advent (late November and December) was sufficient preparation for people to understand Jesus and discern mission. In the contemporary pagan world, that preparation time must be extended. In North America, it will take all of autumn to study the prophets and other faithful Old Testament servants.

In Australia, these months will more likely be February through July. Christmas is doubtless important, but Easter remains the Christian Holy Day when seekers, drop outs, and marginal members are most likely to return to the church. This is the day more likely to define the person and work of Christ, and the period to discern and understand the Christian's mission will extend into June and July. The Disciple Cycle in Australia, therefore, will offset the schedule by about three months. The first story line will begin in August rather than May. This in turn requires some additional changes to the pattern of study at Christmas. Several passages from the story line of "Christ's Purpose" (surrounding Easter) have been moved to Christmas and integrated into the story line of "David's Legacy." This makes good theological sense, and also adapts well to the Australian calendar.

The strategy of worship theme, team meditation, and small-group discussion should connect very well with Australian church experience. The churches tend to be smaller, intimacy and trusted dialogue tend to be even more important, and lay leadership development is an even higher priority. It is even more crucial in Australia that the declining numbers of clergy mentor laity into the spiritual leadership of the church.

I am indebted in writing this appendix to Robin Trebilcock, a pastor with the Uniting Church Australia and author of *The Small Church at Large: Being Local in a Global Context* (Abingdon Press, 2003).

The Uncommon Lectionary: Disciple Cycle

Overall Strategy

1. Weeks are numbered 1 to 52. Designated months may vary as some months have five Sundays. Keep following the numbered weeks.
2. The cycle starts with week 19 at the beginning of the first story line, and follows a calendar most relevant to the pace of contemporary culture.
3. There are five major story lines for worship teaching and small-group discussion. Review all the texts for small-group exploration.
4. Orient worship to coach faith, hope, or lifestyle as the Spirit leads. Try to diversify the focus through the year. Add to the primary text as called.
5. Ground worship in the experience of Jesus as the Spirit leads. Try to diversify the focus through the year.

Design of Worship

1. Build on the basic text using sources from the small-group study.
2. Focus the worship around faith, hope, or lifestyle.
3. Combine drama, music, and image with the spoken word.
4. Link with small-group discussion.

Preparation of the Worship Design Team

1. Feel absolutely free to think, consult, and create!
2. Review the core values, beliefs, vision, and mission of the church.
3. Ground the worship in the experience of Christ.
4. Link with training small-group leaders.

Preparation for Small Groups

1. Read all the texts ahead of time.
2. Set the texts in the overall context of the story line.
3. Select specific parts of the story or specific texts for focus this year, depending on faith, hope, or lifestyle coaching and the key experience of Christ in worship.

Evaluation

- Has the worship effectively communicated faith, or inspired hope, or shaped lifestyle for the participants?
- Has the worship helped participants experience Jesus Christ?
- Has the worship informed and enhanced small-group discussion during the week?

The Uncommon Lectionary: Disciple Cycle for Australia

Week	Worship Theme	Faith, Hope, Lifestyle	Worship Team Meditation	Way of Christ	Small-Group Study	Story Line
						Israel's Covenant
(August)						
32	Genesis 1:1-31		1 Corinthians 15:20-25, 35-49		Genesis 1–3; 7–8	Creation to Noah
33	Genesis 17:1-21		John 8:39-58		Genesis 15; 17:1–18:15; 21:1-7; 22:1-19	Covenant of Abram; Isaac's Sacrifice
34	Genesis 28:10-22; 32:22-32; 33:1-11		Hebrews 11:1, 8-39; 12:1-14		Genesis 25:19-34; 27; 28:10-22; 32:3–33:16	Jacob's Story
35	Genesis 45:1-28		Mark 3:7-19, 31-35		Genesis 37; 39–50	Joseph's Story
(September)						
36	Exodus 3:1-17		Luke 9:28-50		Exodus 1:1–4:17	Moses' Call
37	Exodus 12:1-39		Matthew 14:1-33		Exodus 4:18–6:13; 6:28–14:31	Passover and Exodus
38	Numbers 20:1-13		John 4:7-42		Numbers 11:1–14:25; 17; 20; 22; 27:12-23	Water from the rock, Balaam's Oracle
39	Deuteronomy 10:12-22; 11:18-21		Romans 7:4-25		Exodus 15; 20; 32; 34; Deuteronomy 10:10–11:32	God's Commandments
(October)						
40	Joshua 24:1-32		Luke 6:27-49		Joshua 1; 20; 23; 24; Judges 5–8; 14–16	Conquest, Re-covenant, Judges

Week	Worship Theme	Faith, Hope, Lifestyle	Worship Team Meditation	Way of Christ	Small-Group Study	Story Line
						David's Legacy
41	Ruth 1:1-17; 4:13-17		John 13:1-20, 31-35		Ruth	David's heritage
42	1 Samuel 1:19-27; 3:1-21		Acts 22:3-21; 26:2-18		1 Samuel 1–3	Call of Samuel
43	1 Samuel 10:14-24		1 Peter 2:1-10		1 Samuel 8–10; 15:10-35	Saul
44	1 Samuel 16:1–17:58		2 Timothy 2:1-15		1 Samuel 16–21; 31	David's struggle with Saul
(November) 45	2 Samuel 7:1-29		1 Timothy 1:12-17; 3:10-13; 6:11-16		2 Samuel 5-7; 11–12; 18	King David
46	Psalms 22; 23		1 Thessalonians 5:1-24		1 Kings 1:1–3:28; 8; Psalms 1; 8; 19; 22; 23; 42; 46; 77	Solomon and the Temple
47	1 Kings 19:1-21		2 Corinthians 11:21–12:10		1 Kings 16:29–22:40	Elijah and Ahab
48	2 Kings 5:1-14		Luke 4:23-30; 17:12-19		2 Kings 2; 4:1–5:19; 13:14-21	Elisha and Naaman
(December) 49	2 Kings 19:20-34; Psalm 137		John 15:1-27		2 Kings 17; 18–20; 25; Psalm 137; 2 Chronicles 36:15-23	Fall of Israel and Judah
50	Isaiah 6:1-8		John 6:41-69		Isaiah 1; 6:1-8; 9; 11	God's call and promises

Week	Worship Theme	Faith, Hope, Lifestyle	Worship Team Meditation	Way of Christ	Small-Group Study	Story Line
51	Colossians 1:1-23		Isaiah 25:1-9; 26:1-3		Luke 1; Colossians 1:13-23	Jesus Messiah and Christ
52	Luke 2:1-20		Isaiah 9:1-7		Matthew 1:18—2:23; Luke 1—2; Philippians 3:1—4:7	The birth of Jesus
						Faithful Servants
(January)						
1	Amos 5:18-24; 7:7-9		Matthew 10:1-42		Amos 1; 5; 7	Justice and God's Plumb Line
2	Hosea 11; 14		Luke 17:1-6; 18:9-17		Hosea 1; 4; 6; 8; 14	Sin and returning to the Lord
3	Micah 5:1-4; 6:1-8		Ephesians 4:1—5:2		Micah 1; 4—7	What the Lord Requires
4	Job 19; 42:1-6		1 Corinthians 15:42-58		Job 1—2; 13—14; 19; 38; 40—42	The problem of evil and suffering
5	Nehemiah 8:1-12		1 Corinthians 1:18-31; 2:1-16; 3:1-23		Ezra; Nehemiah 8; Ecclesiastes 3; Proverbs 8—15	Return of the exiles and true wisdom
(February)						
6	Jeremiah 31:27-34		Luke 14:15-35		Jeremiah 11—13; 17:5-18; 18:1-6; 31:27-34	The Potters Clay and calls to repentance

Week	Worship Theme	Faith, Hope, Lifestyle	Worship Team Meditation	Way of Christ	Small-Group Study	Story Line
7	Isaiah 41:1-13		Philippians 4:4-13		Isaiah 30:1-18; 35; 40–42; 45	God's assurance of love and redemption
8	Isaiah 55:1-13		Romans 10:1-17		Isaiah 52–53; 55; 58:1-9; 61:1-11	God's grace and forgiveness
						<u>Jesus' Purpose</u>
9	Psalms 91; 139		2 Corinthians 4:1-18		Psalms 84; 91; 96; 100; 116; 121; 139	Hope and faithfulness
(March) 10	John 19:16-30; 20:11-18		Isaiah 53:1-12		John 18–20; Matthew 27:1-54; Hebrews 8	The significance of Jesus' death
11	Luke 4:16-30		Isaiah 42:1-9; Psalm 22		Luke 4:16-43; Matthew 5–7; Galatians 5	Jesus' preaching and modeling
12	John 8:12; 9:1-41		Isaiah 60:1-5, 19-22		John 8–10; 1 John 1:5–2:17	Light of the World
13	1 Corinthians 13		Hosea 11:1-4, 8-12		John 14–16; 1 Corinthians 11–14	The love of Jesus
(April) 14	Luke 13:22-30; 15:11-32		Habakkuk 2:1-4; 3:17-19		Luke 13–15; 18; Romans 12	The hope of Jesus

Week	Worship Theme	Faith, Hope, Lifestyle	Worship Team Meditation	Way of Christ	Small-Group Study	Story Line
5	1 Peter 2:1-10		Psalm 27		John 2–5; 1 Peter 1; 1 John 4	The inner meaning of Jesus
6	Mark 4:1-9; 26-41		Ezekiel 34:1-31		Mark 1–5; Ephesians 2	The acts of Jesus
7	Mark 6:30-52		Deuteronomy 10:10–11:7		Mark 6–9; James 1	The teachings of Jesus
8	Mark 10:13-34		Isaiah 11:1-9		Mark 10–13; Romans 8	The significance of Jesus
(May) 9	John 1		Zechariah 9:9-10		John 1; 1 Corinthians 3	The Lordship of Jesus
						Christians' Mission
10	Acts 1:6-11; Matthew 28:16-20		2 Kings 2:1-12		Matthew 28; Luke 24; Acts 1; 1 Peter; 1 John	Great Commission
11	Acts 2:1-13, 37-47		Joel 2:28-29		Luke 14; Acts 2:1–6:7; James; Romans 12–15	First growth of the church
12	Galatians 5:1-25		Isaiah 49:8-13		Acts 8–12; Galatians	Emergence of apostles and outreach
(June) 13	2 Corinthians 4:1–6:13		Jonah		Acts 13:1–15:35; 2 Corinthians	Missionaries in a pagan world

Week	Worship Theme	Faith, Hope, Lifestyle	Worship Team Meditation	Way of Christ	Small-Group Study	Story Line
24	Acts 16		Micah 4:1-7		Acts 15:36—16:40; Philippians	Paradigm church growth
25	John 13:1-35		Isaiah 55:1-13		Acts 17—18; Matthew 25—27; John 6; 13	Eucharist and Gentile mission
26	Ephesians 2:1-22; 6:10-20		Ezekiel 36:37—37:28		Acts 19—20; John 20; 1 Corinthians; Ephesians	Resurrection and explaining salvation
(July) 27	2 Timothy 1:1—2:13; 4:1-5		Proverbs 2:1-22		Acts 21—26; John 21; 1 and 2 Timothy	Leadership in mission
28	Colossians 3:1-17		Psalm 121		Acts 27—28; Colossians	Victory and new life in Christ
29	Romans 1:16-17; 5:1-11		Psalms 42; 56		Romans 1—5; Revelation 1—3	Righteousness by faith
30	Romans 8:1-39		Psalm 51		Romans 7—8; John 11—12; Deuteronomy 5:1—6:9	Law and grace
31	1 Thessalonians 4:1—5:24		Jeremiah 31:7-14; 33:14-16	—	Romans 10—11; 1 Thessalonians; Revelation 21—22	Eternal hope and the end of time